CANNABIS BUSINESS

32 WAYS TO MAKE MONEY

THE SECRET TO
GROW, OPEN and RUN
A MARIJUANA DISPENSARY

OSCAR WHITE

CANNABIS/MARIJUANA BUSINESS INFORMATION ®

The cannabis industry is huge and continues to grow. If you're interested in starting a cannabis business, here's how to start and what to keep in mind.

OSCAR WHITE's focus is to help accelerate the success and acceptance of the legal cannabis market by providing actionable intelligence to **HELP ALL ASPECTS OF THE BUSINESS** – from seed to sale – **SUCCEED AND GROW**. He focuses strictly on the business of legal cannabis for medical and recreational use and aims to provide timely information to help the reader make timely, informed decisions to help them run their business **BETTER AND MORE PROFITABLY.**
© **GLOBALLY!** ©

◆ COFFEE SHOP /DISPENSARIES /GROW SHOP /HEAD SHOP ◆

If you are one of the many entrepreneurs interested in opening a marijuana dispensary, this book can guide you through the necessary steps.

◆ 33 IDEAS TO MAKE MONEY IN THE CANNABIS INDUSTRY ◆

So, how can you get in on this Green Rush? The possibilities are only limited by your creativity. In order to stimulate your imagination, here are 33 ways for people to make money in the cannabis industry RIGHT NOW.

WITH THIS INFORMATION, YOU HAVE A GOOD CHANCE OF OPENING A SUCCESSFUL, LUCRATIVE DISPENSARY!

<u>YOU CAN GET STARTED ON YOUR NEW BUSINESS TODAY!</u>

CONTENTS

INTRODUCTION 10

CHAPTER 1: BRIEF NOTES ON MARIJUANA....................... 14

CHAPTER 2: LEGALIZATION 25

CHAPTER 3: LEGALIZATION IN THE USA............................ 36

    American states where cannabis remains illegal: the red trident.. 41

CHAPTER 4: LIGHT MARIJUANA AND MEDICAL MARIJUANA 44

CHAPTER 5: COFFEE SHOP /DISPENSARIES /GROW SHOP /HEAD SHOP 47

    COFFEESHOP: THE CORE OF DUTCH TOURISM 47
    DISPENSARY: US CANNABIS STORES 49
    COLLECTIVE: NON-PROFIT ORGANIZATIONS 51
    Social clubs in Spain 53

CHAPTER 6: HOW TO GET INTO THE MARIJUANA BUSINESS 56

    How to start a marijuana business in 5 steps 57
    Step 1: decide what type of marijuana business to start 58
    Step 2: write your business plan 59
    Step 3: register the company name 60
    Step 4: register to pay taxes 61
    Step 5: Get funds for your marijuana business 62

CHAPTER 7: HOW TO OBTAIN A LICENSE FOR A MEDICAL MARIJUANA DISPENSARY 64

    Arizona 66
    Arkansas 66
    California.. 67
    Colorado 68

CONNECTICUT	69
DELAWARE	70
FLORIDA	71
HAWAII	72
ILLINOIS	72
IOWA	73
MAIN	74
MARYLAND	75
MICHIGAN	76
MINNESOTA	77
NEVADA	78
NEW HAMPSHIRE	80
NEW JERSEY	81
NEW MEXICO	81
NEW YORK	82
NORTH DAKOTA	82
OHIO	83
OKLAHOMA	84
OREGON	85
RHODE ISLAND	86
TENNESSEE	87
UTAH	88
WASHINGTON	89
WISCONSIN	89

CHAPTER 8: LICENSES IN THE REST OF THE WORLD 92

EUROPE	93
HOW TO OPEN A SOCIAL CLUB	94
Starting a Cannabis Social Club in 4 steps	*95*

CHAPTER 9: LICENSES AND BUREAUCRATIC PROCEDURES IN THE USA 101

THE TRANSITION FROM THE MARKET TO THERAPEUTIC USE	101
LICENSING	102
TAXATION	103
STATE EXCISE AND OTHER TAXES	104
PACKAGING, ADVERTISING AND MARKETING	106

CHAPTER 10: HOW MUCH DOES IT COST TO OPEN A DISPENSARY? **115**

A CANNABIS BUSINESS PLAN (TEAM) CAN CONTROL STARTUP COSTS 120
RECORD-KEEPING PLAN TO PREVENT CANNABIS DIVERSION OR CASH COSTS.. 123
FINANCIAL ABILITY TO DESIGN, BUILD AND MANAGE CANNABIS BUSINESSES 124
EMPLOYEE HANDBOOK AND EDUCATIONAL POLICIES REQUIRED BY ILLINOIS CANNABIS LAW 125
COMMUNITY COMMITMENT / SOCIAL EQUITY PLAN TO ACHIEVE THE GOALS OF THE ILLINOIS CANNABIS LAW 126
COSTS FOR EMPLOYEES OF THE CANNABIS DISPENSARY 126
COSTS FOR YOUR PROFESSIONAL CANNABIS CONSULTANTS......... 127
COSTS TO PROMOTE YOUR CANNABIS BUSINESS 127

CHAPTER 11: HOW TO APPLY FOR A LICENSE IN MASSACHUSETTS **129**

TYPES OF MASSACHUSETTS CANNABIS LICENSES 129

CHAPTER 12: LICENSE FOR HEMP DISTRIBUTOR IN NEW YORK... **134**

ADULT USE DISTRIBUTOR LICENSE RESTRICTIONS..................... 135

CHAPTER 13: WHAT IS A DELIVERY LICENSE? **137**

CHAPTER 14: GEORGIA MEDICAL CANNABIS PRODUCTION LICENSE... **139**

WHAT CANNABIS PRODUCTS CAN A CLASS 1 AND CLASS 2 MEDICAL MARIJUANA LICENSEE PRODUCE? 141
COST OF MEDICAL CANNABIS PRODUCTION LICENSE IN GEORGIA . 141
QUESTIONNAIRE FOR CANDIDATES 142

CHAPTER 15: GETTING A LICENSE IN MISSISSIPPI **145**

TAXES IN MISSISSIPPI FOR MARIJUANA................................... 146

CHAPTER 16: PENNSYLVANIA... **148**

HOW TO OPEN A DISPENSARY IN PENNSYLVANIA 150

HOW TO GET A MICROGROWERS LICENSE IN PENNSYLVANIA? 151

CHAPTER 17: HOW TO GET A LICENSE IN SOUTH DAKOTA 153

TYPES OF MARIJUANA LICENSES TO APPLY FOR IN SOUTH DAKOTA 154
HOW MUCH DOES A MARIJUANA LICENSE COST IN SOUTH DAKOTA?
.... 155
TAXES IN SOUTH DAKOTA FOR MARIJUANA 157
GROWING AT HOME IN SOUTH DAKOTA 158

CHAPTER 18: HOW TO GET A LICENSE IN FRESNO IN CALIFORNIA 161

CHAPTER 19: HOW TO OBTAIN A COMMERCIAL LICENSE OF CANNABIS IN MONTANA 168

TYPES OF COMMERCIAL CANNABIS LICENSES IN MONTANA 169
SOCIAL EQUITY PROGRAM IN MONTANA 173
TAXES IN MONTANA FOR CANNABIS 174
KEY POINTS ON MONTANA INITIATIVE I-190 175

CHAPTER 20: HOW TO BECOME A BUDTENDER 177

QUALIFICATIONS / CERTIFICATIONS 179

CHAPTER 21: WORKING WITH CANNABIS 183

HOW TO ENTER THE CANNABIS INDUSTRY 184
THE JOBS IN THE CANNABIS SECTOR, AND HOW MUCH
THEY ARE PAID 187

CHAPTER 22: HOW TO OPEN A CONSUMER ROOM IN DETROIT 196

CHAPTER 23: NEW JERSEY CANNABIS MICRO ENTERPRISE LICENSE 198

TYPES OF CANNABIS MICRO - ENTERPRISE LICENSES IN NEW JERSEY
.... 200

CHAPTER 24: GROWING MARIJUANA 202

GROWING MARIJUANA IN CANADA 203
Production 204

Sale 205
Provinces / Territories Age limit.............................. 206
Marketing and design... 210
Consumption and possession................................... 211

32 IDEAS TO MAKE MONEY IN THE CANNABIS INDUSTRY
... 213

CANNABIS BUSINESS
OSCAR WHITE

Copyright © 2021 OSCAR WHITE All rights reserved.

No part of this guide may be reproduced in any form without permission in writing from the publisher except in the case of brief quotations embodied in critical chapters or reviews.

Legal & Disclaimer

The information contained in this book and its contents is not designed to replace or take the place of any form of medical or professional advice; and is not meant to replace the need for independent medical, financial, legal or other professional advice or services, as may be required. The content and information in this book have been provided for educational and entertainment purposes only.

The content and information contained in this book has been compiled from sources deemed reliable, and it is accurate to the best of the Author's knowledge, information and belief. However, the Author cannot guarantee its accuracy and validity and cannot be held liable for any errors and/or omissions. Further, changes are periodically made to this book as and when needed. Where appropriate and/or necessary, you must consult a professional (including but not limited to your doctor, attorney, financial advisor or such other professional advisor) before using any of the suggested remedies, techniques, or information in this book.

Upon using the contents and information contained in this book, you agree to hold harmless the Author from and against any damages, costs, and expenses, including any legal fees potentially resulting from the application of any of the information provided by this book. This disclaimer applies to any loss, damages or injury caused by the use and application, whether directly or indirectly, of any advice or information presented, whether for breach of contract, tort, negligence, personal injury, criminal intent, or under any other cause of action.

You agree to accept all risks of using the information presented inside this book.

You agree that by continuing to read this book, where appropriate and/or necessary, you shall consult a professional (including but not limited to your doctor, attorney, or financial advisor or such other advisor as needed) before using any of the suggested remedies, techniques, or information in this book.

INTRODUCTION

Legal cannabis in the United States is the industry that is creating the most jobs ever. Today there are more than 240 thousand full-time jobs in the sector with a record growth of 110% in just 3 years, while a study argues that if all 50 states had made it legal, they could have already exceeded one million by today.

Legalizing cannabis economically means creating jobs. And not just by a little, if you look at the real data coming from the United States and the projections made by analysts. According to a recent report by New Frontier Data, under full federal legalization, jobs could have been 1.46 million in 2019, to over 1.6 million in 2025.

The data collected by Leafly analysts, who publish an annual report on the subject, tells us that in January 2020, 243,700 full-time workers connected to the sector were 243,700, which becomes 340,000 including those part-time, according to New Frontier.

Even in a difficult year for the sector, such as 2019, nearly 34,000 new full-time jobs were created. An increase that in 2018 amounted to 68 thousand new places. In general, from about 122 thousand jobs in 2017, it has gone to 240 thousand at the end of 2019, incredible growth, if compared to other sectors. In fact, cannabis grew by more than 110% in just 3 years and, to give an example, 100% growth is expected for the sector of solar panel installers in the USA, but in ten years, not in 3.

According to experts: *"The cannabis industry suffered its first growing pains in 2019. The irrational exuberance of 2018 has given way to the reality of a slow-growing Canadian market, shrinking investment capital, the health crisis, which is fading, and the layoffs of some of the leading brands in the sector".*
But: "*These setbacks were more than offset by tremendous growth in new markets like Massachusetts, Oklahoma and Florida.*"

California, despite a troubled 2019 due to the fact that the post-legalization situation in the country that started in 2018 is settling down, remains the largest legal employer of cannabis in America. But it is Colorado where there is the highest number of cannnabis jobs per capita with one job for every 165 residents. Meanwhile, Colorado continues to overtake the state of Washington. Both states legalized cannabis in 2012, but Colorado's industry boasts nearly 10,000 more jobs than Washington, even though Washington has nearly two million more residents.

Overall, according to Ian Siegel, CEO of the employment agency ZipRecruiter.com, the vacancies related to this new industry grew by 445% from 2017 to 2018 and by over 200% in 2019. The same agency in February 2019 has at least 1,400 open positions, ranging from laboratory technician in Adelanto, California, with an hourly wage of between $ 14 and $ 16, or technicians for the extraction of active ingredients who could aim for an inclusive annual salary between 40 thousand and 60 thousand dollars, which would become between 65 and 90 thousand a year for the role of Extraction Lab Manager.

In short, well-defined and above all well-paid positions, precisely because they require excellent preparation and a necessary specialization that is going hand in hand with the growth of the market.

After all, last year's projections were more than positive: by 2026 the value of the American market for legal cannabis could grow by 50 billion dollars, according to Bloomberg.

In 2016 alone, sales in Canada and the United States grew by 30%, for a total market value of $ 6.7 billion. Unprecedented growth. Specifically, the market is growing along two main segments: as for medical cannabis, sales will increase and bring the market value to 13.3 billion by 2020, while estimates for recreational cannabis project an overall sales value of $ 11.2 billion within four years.

In Europe, too, we are moving towards more liberal policies and this will create new opportunities for work and income for the most enterprising people. In these pages we will explain what these new job opportunities are and how to take advantage of them.

CHAPTER 1: BRIEF NOTES ON MARIJUANA

We are in 2020 and everyone knows what marijuana is and its properties. Now more than ever, preconceptions and prejudices towards this substance are gradually collapsing: consequently, tolerance increases.

Many are literally falling in love with it and celebrities are certainly no exception: just think of the famous rapper Snoop Dogg who, after being an avid supporter of marijuana consumption for years, advertising his innate passion for good weed, without making it secret, has chosen to be an integral part of this sector, inaugurating its own cannabis brand, "Leaves of Snoop".

He therefore appears as a character with a marked entrepreneurial intelligence, since he has chosen to invest in a sector that in the next ten years, according to statistics, should undergo an exponential increase in terms of growth.

Therefore, whether it is to take CBD oil or medical cannabis, the consumption of marijuana involves millions of people around the world, and it just seems not to want to stop. Here is everything you need to know about marijuana and its derivatives.

Marijuana, often referred to alternatively by terms such as weed, ganja or kief, is the plant matter characterized by the inflorescences produced by female cannabis sativa plants.

These flowering tops are generally harvested at the end of the summer season and then dried and subsequently cut in such a way as to allow them to be enjoyed.

It generally looks like a sort of green, brown or greyish "shredded" material: alternatively, the inflorescences are kept unaltered, especially if of high quality.

The traditional Indian expression " bhang ", however particularly widespread, identifies a less valuable plant material, generally offered at lower cost, characterized only by the leaves of the cannabis plant or alternatively, a sort of herbal tea with marijuana, a particular hot drink which, in addition to hemp, contains aromatic herbs, spices and fruit extracts.

The presence of seeds in marijuana is generally synonymous with the poor quality of the strain used in cultivation, as well as the lack of care on the part of the grower who in this case did not promptly separate the male from the female specimens.

Much appreciated by connoisseurs, the so-called " sensimilla" appears, from the name of a particularly intense Californian marijuana variety, obtained through a careful selection of genetics and which does not have any seeds inside the inflorescence. And this is just an example, since the countless varieties of marijuana available are often defined by fancy names that in some way help to further attract the consumer: White Widow, Orange Bud, Purple Haze, Lemon Haze, Amnesia Haze and even Super Skunk, undoubtedly appear among the best known and sold in the main weed shops, the same ones that can be taken with the use of a bong or by rolling a simple joint.

The concentration of legal CBD, as well as THC in marijuana is extremely variable. In general, the presence of tetrahydrocannabinol is between 1 and 7%, although there are varieties of marijuana that can easily reach 20 or 22%: in recent years there has been a considerable increase in THC levels. of marijuana, the psychotropic and psychoactive active ingredient. This change is mainly due to the improvement of cultivation methods and the production of new varieties and hybridizations. Marijuana habitually taken today is up to 5 times more potent than that consumed at the end of the 70s, and this helps to promote the interest of those who want to perceive pleasant and invigorating sensations.

The success of marijuana is mainly due to this: it is a cerebral and bodily "drug" that, if taken in moderation, stimulates creativity, gives energy and brings significant benefits to the body, by virtue of the presence of CBD or cannabidiol with markedly relaxing and soothing effects.

There are basically three types of marijuana commonly found in nature, identified specifically in hemp sativa, indica and ruderalis.

Marijuana or cannabis sativa, is typical of tropical, warm and humid areas such as Mexico, Colombia, India and North Africa. The plants can easily reach five meters in height and have abundant and large leaves. Known for its cerebral effects, it is stimulating and euphoric and its use is indicated if you undertake activities that involve the use of inspiration and creativity.

Marijuana derived from cannabis indica, on the other hand, is native to colder areas, such as those of the Himalayas, and plants prefer light while tolerating drought. The plant appears rather squat, with nodules and branches that tend to intertwine along the stem, reaching about one and a half meters in height. The inflorescences, on the other hand, are dense and concentrated, responsible for the predominantly corporeal, sedative and relaxing effect, so much so that they are also used for therapeutic purposes to relieve joint and muscle pain, migraines or in the treatment of chronic pain in the case of therapeutic cannabis.

Marijuana belonging to the ruderalis species is instead typical of the Siberian areas: it is distinguished by the reduced height of the plants and the small size of the leaves, which are palmate and serrated.

Particularly resistant to very harsh climates, it shows the ability to spread spontaneously wherever land is available: it is in fact easy to find it in nature, grouped in dense expanses.

It turns out to be the most used variety in order to obtain hybrid genetics with high concentrations of CBD, from which countless derivatives are produced, aimed at guaranteeing the well-being of the body.

This is the case of medical cannabis, successfully used in recent years as a valid substitute for conventional pharmacological therapies against chronic pain, where the latter have not had the desired effects, as well as light hemp with a reduced THC content, limited to a concentration equal to 0.2%, with a tolerance margin of up to 0.6%.

Unmistakable from an anatomical point of view, the marijuana plant can vary its morphology according to the species it belongs to. Generally, it can appear as a sort of bush from about one meter to one and a half meters high, or alternatively take on a slenderer appearance, accompanied by considerable heights, even exceeding 2 meters.

Each plant obviously has a root system, consisting of a single tap root, which grows below the surface of the soil and which serves to promote the absorption of nutrients, representing a sort of anchor.

Emerging from the roots is the main stem which allows the marijuana plant to grow vertically. It is in fact the primary vascular channel, the same one that carries water and minerals from the roots while the secondary branches grow from the main stem, through points called nodes.

Branching involves the formation of a pair of branches starting from each node, on both sides of the stem. The distance between branches by definition takes on the expression of "internodal space". Generally, indica-dominant strains have a smaller internodal space than sativa-dominant strains. From the branches come out the characteristic palmate leaves, a significant and unmistakable emblem of marijuana.

Marijuana leaves are called palmate or alternatively called "fan": they have a symmetrical structure and grow in pairs, starting from both the main stem and the relative branches.

The characteristic fan leaves distinguish an indica hemp plant from sativa. In general, particularly dark and broad leaves are typical of indica, if light green in color with thin, long and tapering "fingers" identify the cannabis sativa varieties. Hybrids usually mix both characteristics.

This form is quite functional for the marijuana plant: each leaf acts as a real "solar panel", absorbing the available light and allowing the phloem or tissue to convey energy and nutritional elements to the entire plant, behaving in fact like a real "electrical system". Fan leaves are also fundamental for photosynthesis: for this reason, they should never undergo too aggressive pruning. Some leaves can be removed in the final phase of flowering if they involve excessive shade and prevent the passage of light to the buds below.

Legal marijuana, weed, cannabis, hemp: these are all terminologies that in fact identify the same substance or plant material. However, this nomenclature includes some subtle differences.

When we talk about cannabis, we refer to the entire hemp plant, sativa or indica, including inflorescences, foliage and stem. The term marijuana specifically indicates dried female inflorescences ready to be taken by means of a bong or simply by rolling a joint, once the plant matter has been mixed with tobacco.

Hemp leaves, also part of the cannabis plant, can be used to make edibles or delicious marijuana herbal teas. There are countless benefits and effects given by marijuana.

Primary is the sense of peace and euphoria characterized above all by the presence of THC or tetracannabinol, a psychotropic and physical active ingredient. By virtue of the often-high concentration of legal CBD or cannabidiol, marijuana helps to promote relaxation, reduce anxiety, insomnia and depression and treat chronic pain caused by autoimmune diseases such as multiple sclerosis and panic attacks. At the same time, it proves to be an effective anti-inflammatory and pain reliever, helping to fight aging, thanks to its well-known antioxidant and anti-radical properties.

The side effects of excessive marijuana use typically consist of drowsiness, altered spatial-temporal perception and mobility, nausea, red eyes, agitation, dry mouth, and decreased blood pressure. However, these often-unpleasant effects tend to disappear quickly and completely spontaneously.

However, the state induced by marijuana can vary considerably depending on the personality of the user, the relative psychological state, the methods of use and the quantity of active ingredients taken. The greatest risk remains undoubtedly cannabis addiction, caused by excessive use of plant matter, thanks to the massive presence of THC in the blood.

With regard to the probable damage to health for those who regularly take marijuana, the main scientific research on the matter confirms that in general this substance appears less harmful than other drugs, this since no death has never been established with certainty caused by an overdose of cannabis.

However, the well-known and appreciated vegetable matter may not turn out to be as harmless as we are led to think: habitual smokers are subjected to the risk of contracting bronchitis more easily, combined with other symptoms affecting the respiratory system.

In the same way, pregnant women who take cannabis are also more likely to give birth to children of less than normal weight: here marijuana in pregnancy is strongly discouraged. In general, according to some studies, those who habitually consume marijuana would be subjected to a higher risk of exacerbating any schizophrenia, psychosis and paranoia.

However, less convincing evidence suggests that marijuana is responsible for worsening certain diseases that have sometimes been associated with consumption, such as testicular cancer or angina pectoris.

At the same time, marijuana intake at school age could affect learning, memory and attention, although to date there is no particular evidence.

On the other hand, no correlation with cancers commonly associated with cigarette smoking, such as those of the lung, asthma and cardiovascular diseases has been found.

A conscious consumption of marijuana can therefore do nothing but bring benefits, in the face of scientific progress that testifies to its countless advantages and benefits, especially when it comes to therapeutic cannabis.

CHAPTER 2: LEGALIZATION

The roots, in a broad sense but also literally, of this infamous plant that is hemp, are to be found in the Asian continent, where it is believed that it was first found.

The oldest evidence of human use dates back to 3000 BC: we are talking about the remains of burnt seeds, found in Central Asia, in the territory of present-day Siberia and in some caves in Romania. Other evidence of its use is scattered through the history of many peoples of ancient times, including the Assyrians, the Chinese, the Arians, the Greeks (not so much in use but in trade).

Herodotus, before the year zero, wrote that the Scythians cultivated and used the cannabis plant, while some Mediterranean populations used to throw it into the fire and get drunk with its scents. It is very likely that the first property discovered by man was the textile one: for thousands of years its fibers have been woven for the production of fabrics.
Just think of the sails of the ships of the ancient Phoenicians which were made up of textile hemp sativa fibers.

In Asia and the Middle East, it had been cultivated for millennia before Christ, while its advent in Europe, through trade, was only a few centuries before the year zero.

The oldest European find is an urn containing seeds and leaves, found in Berlin, which dates back to around 500 BC. and in any case more or less from that time its cultivation spread to the old continent.

In America, on the other hand, it seems that it was introduced by the post-Columbus colonization (1492 AD), even if many doubts about it remain due to findings in some Peruvian tombs of 1500 BC.

The cannabis plant has ancient origins, about 12,000 years of history proven by scientific findings found by man, especially in various areas of the Asian continent.

It is probable that from here, especially thanks to the commercial traffic of the "Silk Road", hemp was known and imported by European merchants who ventured beyond their borders.

In Italy, for example, the first imports took place in the Maritime Republics, thanks to the commercial exchanges that these cities lived on.

In Europe, the cultivation of hemp was very successful, as many areas (including Italy) were well suited for both climate and soil type.

Its use was mostly textiles, for the production of ropes and fabrics but also paper, seed oil, animal feed and much more.

The famous Gutenberg Bible, the first book in Europe to be printed with movable type, dating back to 1453, was in fact made of hemp paper.

In the 1900s its use was still widespread, also by virtue of the great wars, for which cannabis, together with other plants, was used for the production of nitrocellulose-based explosive devices.

More noble purposes were pursued by Henry Ford, who in the 1930s launched the prototype of the Hemp Body Car, a car built partially of hemp fiber and which used hemp ethanol as fuel.

History teaches us that economic interests can turn a state, or the whole world, in an instant and this happened to cannabis and its eco-friendly reputation.

It seems that it was because of the American Hearst, leader in the manufacture of paper derived from wood, that cannabis was slowly discriminated against.

The aim was to put the plant in a bad light for its psychoactive effects, in order to clear the way for the fortunes of the new wooden paper.

The term "marijuana" was born in this period, a deliberately Mexican name, and was used as an expedient and the cause of some heinous crimes of the time.

Obviously, it was instrumentalized journalism, aimed at putting Mexico (then a rival of the USA in a border war closed a few years earlier) and therefore marijuana, in a bad light.

In 1937 came the first law against the cultivation and use of hemp, after it was communicated to the public that the relaxing drug "Cannabis" contained marijuana.

From here on, in the US and around the world, hemp began to be demonized.

Discrimination against hemp continued throughout the 1900s. In the 1960s, for example, marijuana was used as a pretext to persecute counterculture movements. All over the world marijuana was prosecuted, it appeared in the lists of drugs as dangerous as heroin and cocaine. But in recent years the debate has reopened, especially thanks to scientific studies that have revealed how marijuana can be useful in the treatment of many diseases ranging from multiple sclerosis, to anorexia, to the treatment of glaucoma, to Parkinson's disease, and don't forget how marijuana serves to mitigate the negative effects of chemotherapy.

Thanks to the scientific evidence of its benefits, many states have begun to legalize the therapeutic use of marijuana, and subsequently many discussions have also been opened on its recreational use. Despite the fact that marijuana has been considered illegal almost all over the world, its consumption has never decreased. For example, the 2017 UN drug report reveals that 188 million people used cannabis in 2017, with production coming from 159 different countries and, mainly, from the Maghreb, Mashrek and the southern Balkans. A number that makes you think this is the most widely used substance in the world, with a growth trend in North America (plus 60% from 2007 to 2017) and in Asia. The Americas are also where the substance is seized the most.

South America represented 38% of the world total in 2017, while North America 21%, a figure in sharp decline compared to 2016 mainly due to the effect of the legalization for non-medical use of the substance in some states. The trend also suggests an increase in both indoor and outdoor growing, with indoor growing closely associated with an overall increase in THC levels compared to two decades ago.
Furthermore, in the last decade, cannabis products have increased, which tend to be rich in THC (one

of the best-known active ingredients in cannabis) and low in CBD. In Europe alone, the average THC content of cannabis resin has doubled from around 8 per cent in 2006 to 17 percent in 2016, and the THC content of cannabis herbs has increased from 5 to 10 per cent over the same period. So legalizing this market means taking away huge profits for criminal organizations. It also means preventing the consumer from coming into contact with criminal circles and protecting his health. Indeed, having legally produced marijuana means for the user to actually know what he is smoking. In the last few years more tolerant policies have been brought forward, if not legalizing marijuana, and this is the situation in the world.

Uruguay will be remembered in the history books as the first state to have fully legalized the recreational use of marijuana: in 2013, causing a media hype and a bitter global debate, President Jose Mujica signs a law which, thanks to subsequent changes, leads the country to be the first nation in the world where it is possible to freely produce, buy and consume hemp. But don't rush to buy a plane ticket to Montevideo: the use of cannabis for recreational purposes is only allowed to Uruguayan citizens and residents, who must be registered in the national register of consumers.

In Canada, the legalization of hemp came in 2018 thanks to the Cannabis Act, which finally allows its recreational use to all citizens of age. In some provinces, marijuana can only be purchased from state-owned companies, while in others it is also legal to buy from individuals. Smoking marijuana is only allowed in private homes, although outdoor use and public parks are tolerated in some provinces. On the contrary, Canadian law harshly prosecutes those who drive while intoxicated: if you are stopped by the police, you may be tested to verify that the THC nanograms contained in your blood do not exceed the 5 established by law. Indoor cultivation is almost always allowed as long as there are no more than 4 plants and strict protocols are followed to prevent children from coming into contact with cannabis.

The landscape of states that are slowly moving towards more permissive legislation, but have not yet made the big leap towards full legalization, is much broader. Here the situation is really confusing and each country has adopted its own laws, with more or less paradoxical aspects. We will see more in a separate chapter.

The country most open to marijuana smokers, but also the one with the most schizophrenic legislation, is Holland. Contrary to what many of you think, cannabis is illegal in the Netherlands, although its use is tolerated nationally. Strange, right? But if it sounds strange to you, wait until you hear what the real "backdoor problem" is, as the Dutch call it: as everyone knows, Holland is home to coffeeshops, but these companies have to source from the black market. In practice, what they buy illegally suddenly becomes legally marketable from the moment it arrives at their facility. Crazy? Yes, and this is why, after a brief period of tightening of the laws, which led to the closure of many coffeeshops, the situation is back as it was before and it seems quite obvious that, sooner or later, the government will legalize what has been done for a long time.

In the rest of Europe, the situation remains very varied. Although many states have opened up to the consumption of light hemp and cannabis for therapeutic purposes, recreational use remains severely repressed. In some countries, such as Spain, the Czech Republic and Switzerland, the legalization process is further ahead than in others and, although not legalized, the possession of hemp is tolerated and decriminalized, as long as the quantity is within the limits set by law.

In the rest of Europe, if you want to buy cannabis, you do it at your own risk: possession of hemp, if it falls within the so-called moderate quantity, is often tolerated by law enforcement, but it is always better not to rely on it. In practice, holding, selling and growing marijuana remains a crime and penalties vary enormously from one country to another.

In the rest of the world, hemp remains totally illegal and penalties for offenders can reach up to life imprisonment, in the case of the purchase and sale of large quantities. The paradoxical aspect of this type of legislation lies in the fact that it is adopted by the countries traditionally producers and consumers of this plant. The quality of Indian and Nepalese hemp is famous all over the world, yet in these states the law is clear: production, possession and trade are totally prohibited. Just as the penalties are very severe in Malaysia, Indonesia and all of South Asia, countries where the possession of a few grams of marijuana can lead to very long detention, not to mention international drug trafficking, for which the penalties come quickly to life imprisonment.

Hemp in Africa is illegal everywhere and while it is true that in many countries it is very easy to find it, be careful what you do: the police are usually ok with the locals, but it is very likely that they are not with you. The only exception on the black continent is South Africa, which in recent years has tried the difficult road to legalization, starting to decriminalize the possession of small quantities and the cultivation of cannabis within its own home.

The war that America began nearly a century ago is not over yet and, although encouraging signs are seen here and there, the road to the complete rehabilitation of hemp is still very long and full of obstacles. But, as often happens, the positions of governments are always much more backward than those of the voters: popular consensus towards a decisive legalization of hemp is increasingly broad and it is not excluded that, in the coming years, many countries will find themselves having to make deals with the anti-prohibitionist pressures of millions of citizens, finally allowing the recreational use of a plant that has not received the treatment it deserved.

However, the situation is in constant ferment and debates continuous, also because the 2 December 2020, the Committee on Narcotic Drugs of the United Nations (UN) voted to remove cannabis from the list of narcotics risky to health, recognizing the therapeutic value. The whole

European Union voted in favor, with the sole exception of Hungary.

The long-awaited decision was taken by the UN based on a series of recommendations from the World Health Organization, of which one in particular was accepted: that relating to the removal of cannabis from Schedule IV attached to the Single Convention on Narcotic Drugs, 1961, where it was listed along with dangerous and highly addictive opioids, such as heroin.

CHAPTER 3: LEGALIZATION IN THE USA

The United States is characterized by a strong paradox: in the USA, prohibition against the consumption of cannabis started with the Marijuana Tax Act approved in 1937 by President Franklin D. Roosevelt.

The legalization movement also started in the United States, with the decision of California, in 1996, to legalize its therapeutic use.
As with prohibition, the legalization movement also spread to the rest of the world.
In 2012, a referendum was held in the states of Colorado and Washington to make the consumption of marijuana legal even for recreational purposes: the decision to legalize cannabis has since fallen entirely into the hands of individual states while in general the consumption of marijuana remains illegal at the federal level, creating many problems.

US states where smoking marijuana is completely legal
The 2012 referendum in Colorado and Washington brought a breath of fresh air to the landscape of pro-legalization movements, representing the first

and real success in the reintegration and restoration of a pre- prohibitionist situation, where the production, sale and marijuana consumption was not subject to any restrictions and limitations.

Currently the states where cannabis is completely legal are:

Colorado and Washington, as mentioned, following the 2012 referendum;

Alaska, Oregon and Washington DC also held a referendum in 2014, fully legalizing the use and sale of marijuana for recreational purposes;

California, Massachussets, Maine and Nevada joined in the November 2016 referendum;

Vermont was, on the other hand, the ninth state to fully legalize cannabis, and the first in the world to do so through parliament, with the decree of January 2018;

US states where medical use of cannabis is legal
To the nine states in which marijuana is completely legal, there are 25 in which it is legal for therapeutic purposes but not for recreational use.

Of these 25 states, in turn, there are 12 that also allow the medical use of cannabis with a THC content of more than 1%, while 13 limit therapeutic use to light marijuana only.

States with more lax regulation are:

- Montana;
- North Dakota;
- Michigan;
- Pennsylvania;
- New Hampshire;
- New Jersey;
- West Virginia;
- Louisiana;
- Arkansas;
- New Mexico;
- Arizona;

- Hawaii.

Those that, on the other hand, limit medical use to light cannabis only are:

- Texas;
- Oklahoma;
- Alabama;
- Georgia;
- South Carolina;
- Tennessee;
- Kentucky;
- Virginia;
- Indiana;
- Wisconsin;
- Iowa;
- Wyoming;

- Utah.

There are also states where decriminalization processes are leading to a progressive legalization of medical use:

- Florida;
- Mississippi;
- North Carolina;
- Maryland;
- Delaware;
- Connecticut;
- Rhode Island;
- New York;
- Minnesota;
- Illinois;
- Missouri.

Especially in these states the debate on legalization remains particularly active and it is not at all implausible to expect a turn towards full legalization by parliament, as happened recently in Vermont.

American states where cannabis remains illegal: the red trident

There are, however, three states in the US that still oppose strenuous resistance to the legalization movement, preferring to stick to prohibitionist positions:

South Dakota. Despite a strong community in favor of legalization and attempts by the government to pass laws in favor of decriminalization, they have all failed due to lack of participation and public opinion, which was, on the whole, strongly opposed. The latest of these initiatives, the collection of signatures which began in 2017, managed to obtain the approval of just 15,000 citizens, insufficient to hold a referendum;

Kansas, certainly the state where the criminal consequences are harshest: possession of marijuana, in fact, can lead to a fine of at least

2,500 dollars and potential incarceration for a year. The country legally recognizes the CBD oil trade, but since every cannabis-derived product contains even only traces of THC, in reality every hemp derivative is banned by the state;

Idaho, likewise, has seen numerous attempts to initiate a gradual process of legalization but none have ever managed to find favor with the population: the latest motion to legalize CBD oil, in April 2015, ended in a clear refusal of parliament;

To the red trident is then added the state of **Nebraska** which, despite still considering both medical and recreational use of marijuana as illegal, has for years implemented a process of progressive decriminalization of the use and possession of modest quantities of cannabis for personal use, getting much closer to European tolerance policies.

The main difference between the European and American legalization movements consists in the different objective: while, in fact, in the light of the above, it appears clear that legalization in the United States is aimed at liberalizing the use and personal production, also considering cannabis with high THC content as useful for therapeutic purposes.

In Europe, however, there is still a lot of skepticism towards the complete liberalization of marijuana.

Tolerance towards recreational cannabis use affects a few countries and is mostly confined to specific locations (Dutch coffee shops or Spanish clubs).

CHAPTER 4: LIGHT MARIJUANA AND MEDICAL MARIJUANA

As often happens in the scientific field, it was the USA that gave the green light to the legalization of the medical use of cannabis: however, it was not a process that took place at the federal level, but thanks to the initiative of individual states that make up the federation, generating different legislative differences between states.

In the old continent, still firm on prohibitionist policies, only Switzerland has begun to legalize the marketing of inflorescences defined as "cannabis light" due to the low content of tetrahydrocannabinol (THC) which must be less than 1%. These varieties of cannabis, crossed with industrial hemp, made it possible to produce inflorescences that do not have a "playful" effect but which, however, can satisfy the consumer's needs for the other cannabinoids contained in the resin produced by the flower.

What is Medical Cannabis?

Varieties with a high content of delta-9-tetrahydrocannabinol (THC) are called Therapeutic

Cannabis due to their pharmacological effect deriving from high concentrations of cannabinoids present in the phytocomplex. These genetics were made illegal in 1937 by the Marihuana Tax Act which introduced prohibition on cannabis, then extended to the whole world with the international agreements on drug trafficking signed in the 1970s.

In fact, this ban has greatly slowed medical research on medical cannabis, which has only recently been able to fully resume.

Are Therapeutic and Light Cannabis the same thing?

The human body is characterized by an endocannabinoid system divided into CB1 and CB2 connected to internal organs and nervous system: our body naturally produces endocannabinoids and is receptive to the natural cannabinoids produced by the cannabis flower.

The difference between therapeutic and light cannabis is characterized by the content of active ingredients contained in the phytocomplex, to have a therapeutic effect there must be high percentages of cannabinoids, but above all high percentages of THC. the tetrahydrocannabinol is the psychoactive cannabinoid which has the function of activator of many elements of the content. Cannabis light also contains cannabinoids and terpenes, but to a reduced extent and with very low percentages of THC, which limits its activation and consequently its therapeutic effects.

CHAPTER 5: COFFEE SHOP /DISPENSARIES /GROW SHOP /HEAD SHOP

The Dutch coffeeshop cannabis has attracted fans from around the world since the 70s. Dispensaries, on the other hand, have only recently begun to emerge in Canada and the United States. But age is not the only factor that distinguishes these two structures. In this chapter we will show you the difference between dispensaries and coffeeshops, and what can be found in both.

COFFEESHOP: THE CORE OF DUTCH TOURISM

The famous Dutch coffeeshops began in the 1970s, after the government of the Netherlands realized that it was impossible to create a completely drug-free society. Therefore, the government decided to take a more tolerant approach to drugs by focusing on harm reduction, rather than criminalizing drug users and encouraging the emergence of a black market in soft drugs such as cannabis and hashish.

Following this new tolerance policy (or " gedoogbeleid "), the Dutch government legalized the sale of cannabis and hashish through licensed coffeeshops. Today, these shops represent the heart of the Dutch tourism sector, attracting millions of visitors to Amsterdam and other major Dutch cities each year.

Coffee shops can be small and cramped places or flashy establishments like the Bulldog in Amsterdam's Red Light District. The coffeeshop in the center of Amsterdam naturally tend to attract more tourists, while those located in the peripheral areas are frequented mostly by locals. Some stores, such as Boerejongens, offer a luxurious setting and sell exclusive products (such as the full line of Amsterdam Genetics). But in essence, the concept behind every coffeeshop is always the same: anyone can enter and buy a small dose of cannabis.

The quality of the ganja varies by coffeeshop. As always, some locales are targeting tourists, offering lower quality cannabis at inflated prices. Therefore, it is preferable to seek advice from some residents to understand which are the best coffeeshops in the area. In general, Dutch coffeeshops offer a large assortment of good quality cannabis, pre- rolled joints, hash and edibles. It is worth noting that Dutch ganja is very potent, so don't overdo it.

By law, coffeeshops cannot sell alcohol or cigarettes. Furthermore, they cannot sell more than 5g of cannabis per day to a single customer, advertise the sale of drugs, or sell to anyone under the age of 18. A good Dutch coffeeshop also has fruit juices, snacks or sweets, coffee, tea and other soft drinks available. In some coffeeshops there is an air of celebration, while in others there is a more relaxing atmosphere, perfect for reading a book, listening to music or chatting with friends.

If you are not a European citizen, keep this important element in mind: Europeans tend to smoke cannabis mixed with tobacco. Therefore, almost all pre- rolled joints available in Dutch coffeeshops contain tobacco. If you prefer to smoke only cannabis, contact a coffeeshop in your area.

DISPENSARY: US CANNABIS STORES

Cannabis dispensaries represent a novelty that emerged after the legalization of cannabis in American states such as California, Colorado,

Washington, Nevada. These shops are subject to particular regulations and sell very different products from Dutch coffeeshops.

Almost all dispensaries operate as a pharmacy: the customer enters, is served by the budtender and takes away his purchases in a bag. In some California dispensaries, patrons are allowed to consume cannabis inside the venue, but these are exceptions. In most US states where ganja is legal (such as Colorado, Nevada, and Washington), it is forbidden to consume cannabis in public places.

As with coffeeshops, even in dispensaries it is possible to find different types of atmosphere, services, prices and products. Some dispensaries are specifically designed for therapeutic consumers and therefore offer different services than dispensaries which cater only to recreational consumers. There are also facilities that supply both types of customers and use separate points of sale for products for therapeutic and recreational purposes.

Unlike Dutch coffeeshops, dispensaries don't always sell cannabis to any adult. Some are allowed to sell cannabis exclusively to state residents, or only to registered patients or medical users. Sometimes it is possible to complete the registration directly on site, or before proceeding with the purchase of products. It all depends on the laws in force in that state.

A good dispensary will offer personalized services to help the customer find the cannabis-containing product that best suits their needs. The dispensaries must be clean and tidy, the budtender must welcome the customers with professionalism and manage the products with equal competence. The assortment of products in a dispensary may vary. However, each venue should always offer a wide selection of flowers, concentrates, vape pens and edibles. Some facilities also sell clones, growing equipment and seeds.

COLLECTIVE: NON-PROFIT ORGANIZATIONS

Cannabis collectives differ from dispensaries in that they are usually non-profit organizations. Like existing collectives in other sectors, these organizations are made up of a group of people working towards a common goal, which is to supply cannabis to those in need for therapeutic reasons or to adult buyers.

Collectives of this type usually offer the same products as dispensaries. However, in some cases, they can only sell cannabis to their own members or to patients registered within the collective, it all depends on the local laws in which the organization operates.

A growshop is a shop specializing in articles and equipment for cultivation and gardening with an eye to the world of hemp.
Among these are the headshops (sale of items for smokers, i.e. lighters, ashtrays, rolling papers, chillums, hookahs, bongs and vaporizers), hempshops (sale of articles and products relating to hemp or derivatives-made with it (clothing, cosmetics, foods, books, magazines, DVDs, etc.), the Smartshops (selling legal psychoactive substances such as supplements or natural and synthetic compounds) and Seedshop (sale of cannabis seeds.) the hemp shop, among the most controversial activities that were born in recent years in the hemp sector, are shops specialized in the sale of articles and products relating to hemp or made with the latter.

In the hemp shop you can find gadgets, objects and clothing, books and information, magazines on the properties and cultivation of hemp, food and drinks (beers, wines, juices, soft drinks, coffee) flavored with cannabis with THC within the limits as well as cosmetics made with this plant with innumerable properties.

The hemp contained in the products sold in the hemp shops is called "sativa".
Sativa hemp has many beneficial properties, used for millennia in many different cultures and parts of the world as a healing plant. Hemp-based cosmetics and creams, for example, have various beneficial properties for the body and the skin.
Even the restaurant sector has reevaluated hemp, which has recently found new industrial and culinary uses with the creation, using hemp flowers or seeds, of oils rich in vitamins, milk, flour, sweets and drinks, all suitable even to those who follow a vegan or gluten-free diet.
Often a growshop is all this and much more: reference points for hemp lovers, info points and food tasting corners.

Social clubs in spain

There are more and more "Associations " dedicated to Marijuana in Spain, the so-called Cannabis Social Clubs.
Introduced by ENCOD, a European network of organizations and companies, which aims to defend the right of citizens to consume certain

substances safely and to raise awareness about cultivation for personal use.

Each "member" must have a card in order to access.

These associations were founded to defend the rights of consumers and to propose actions and policies on Cannabis, on legalization and on the benefit that society could have.

Each member can purchase a few grams of weed or hash a day for personal use.

This should be consumed within the Cannabis Social Club, an environment that guarantees security and privacy, but many often buy it to take it and consume it at home: however, remember that in public places it is strictly forbidden to consume marijuana or derivatives.

This policy is aimed at the prevention and reduction of harm, especially as regards minors and those most at risk.

What do you find in a cannabis social club?

There are different kinds of "associations", and also depends on the climate and the number of members of the Club. In Spain there are hot spots almost all year round like the Canaries and more cooler places in northern Spain.

You can find Cannabis Social Clubs with open spaces, tables and sofas, or even simple large rooms with chairs and there are elements that are found in almost all Cannabis clubs.

For example, you can always find the classic counter with the precision balance, the cards are provided for the members and which will guarantee them their daily quantity of cannabis.

Also inside there is always a bar for members or vending machines with drinks and snacks. Inevitably present are video game consoles, such as PS, Xbox, or table football, useful for socializing and spending time with other kids.

Sometimes you can also find a corner with books, a space dedicated to reading, or simply areas to make friends.

CHAPTER 6: HOW TO GET INTO THE MARIJUANA BUSINESS

In some US countries, marijuana is completely illegal. But in 38 states in the United States, it is both recreationally and medically legal. This means that the demand for marijuana is high and it is a relatively new industry to legally enter if you are considering starting a business.

With its age and regulatory environment, the cannabis industry is unlike any other. Entrepreneurs need to think about entering the market with a marijuana business. Here's what you need to know before starting a marijuana business and the steps to take if you decide to enter the cannabis industry.

What does the marijuana industry look like today?

Before starting any business, you should have an idea of what the industry landscape is like.

What are the earning potentials? What are the risks? Who is your competition? These are all unknowns that you would like to have a check on before starting a marijuana business. Given the short history of the marijuana industry, no one can be fully sure how the cannabis industry will turn out and how the marijuana companies will fare. An important aspect to consider is the question in your area where you plan to start your marijuana business and how you can distinguish yourself from others offering the same service. After all, you won't be the only one wondering how to start a marijuana business.

As more and more states legalize drugs, marijuana companies have greater earning potential. Since legalization in 2014, the regulated sales of the cannabis industry in Colorado have exceeded $ 6 billion. And sales are projected to reach $ 50 billion by 2026, further demonstrating the potential of a profitable industry.

How to start a marijuana business in 5 steps

There is no denying that the cannabis industry can be a profitable career choice. But starting a business, any business, requires a fair amount of work, both to prepare it and to legally set up and run it. If you are wondering how to start a marijuana business, these six steps can guide you through the process. Let's begin.

Step 1: decide what type of marijuana business to start

Normally, the first step to starting a business would be to have a business idea, but if you're ready to start a marijuana business, you've already completed that step. What you need to decide is which part of the marijuana business you want to be involved in. Do you want to open a dispensary, grow marijuana or deliver it? Maybe you want to do it all. The steps to starting a marijuana business cannot progress until you have decided on this aspect.

Many of the other steps to starting a business will be pretty basic, but remember that with marijuana-related businesses the laws can change dramatically from state to state and you need to be very sure of them before taking action. You will need to spend a lot of time on your research so that you fully understand the rules on where and how you can sell marijuana. Talking to people who have started their own cannabis businesses is also a good place to start.

Step 2: write your business plan

As with any business, you need a business plan before you can start doing anything else. When starting a marijuana business, the plan will need to be a little more detailed than it would be if you opened a less regulated business like a restaurant or jewelry business.

First of all, make sure you follow all laws in your state. Where do you want to open your marijuana business to who your suppliers will be, make sure everything is in line with the law.

"The most surprising thing about having a cannabis business is the amount of regulation that is involved and the way it is constantly changing," said Dr. Jared Helfant, president of Sparx Cannabis. Helfant 's business is based in California, the first state to legalize and where today marijuana is legal for both medical and recreational use.

Your business plan will likely continue to change as the laws do, but it is vital that you have it in place when you first start a cannabis business. When creating your first business plan, make sure it includes:

- Business costs and when you expect to make a profit;

- How do you intend to attract customers;

- What will distinguish your business from other similar ones and who your competitors are;

- Where will you run your business from;

- Who will your suppliers be;

- If you already have legal counsel, to help you keep everything in order.

Step 3: register the company name

Because marijuana is not federally legalized and national prohibitions prevent the interstate sale of cannabis, large companies have generally been away from the cannabis industry until now, making it a prime sector for local business entry.

Your marijuana business will likely be local and on a smaller scale, but you still need to choose a business entity that is right for you. The business entity you choose will affect the taxes you pay and the level of risk you are exposed to. You may be inclined to open your business as a limited liability company, also called an LLC, or perhaps a corporation. Both entities can protect owners from personal liability, but there are some key differences when it comes to LLCs and corporations.

You will also need to choose a name for your marijuana business. The process for choosing a business name will be specific to your state, but typically you'll need to do a search to make sure the name you want is available, so there will be a small fee associated with booking your name for a fixed amount of time. Establish both of these things before trying to register your marijuana business, as you will need this information to do so.

Step 4: register to pay taxes

As with all the other steps in our guide on how to start a marijuana business guide, this will differ depending on the state in which you are starting your marijuana business. However, regardless of where you are starting your cannabis business, you should apply for an employer identification number, which is also sometimes called a corporate tax number.

You can apply for an EIN online directly from the IRS and get approved almost immediately. You will need it as tax season approaches and you are looking to pay wages and income taxes for your business. Your EIN will also be required if you decide to open a corporate bank account or credit card or apply for a loan. Which brings us to our next step

Step 5: Get funds for your marijuana business

Every new entrepreneur faces the reality of the costs of starting a business. Those who start a marijuana business, however, may have more expenses than a typical business. And if you find that you can't cover all these upfront costs yourself, you might be looking for funding to start your own marijuana business. This is another reason why you want to create a comprehensive business plan - any investor or lender you go looking for money to will want to see it to know if your marijuana business is well thought out and that you have a plan to make a profit. And when you start thinking about financing.

As mentioned above, as a dispensary, you will need licenses to sell medical marijuana. In states where medical marijuana is legal, marijuana companies typically have to pay a non-refundable membership fee of approximately $ 5,000 to start the business. (In Louisiana it costs only $ 150 to apply, but in New Jersey it is $ 20,000.) Most certificate applicants fail to meet the initial capital requirements needed to ensure smooth operations from the start.

The applications and licensing fees, coupled with any regular equipment, marketing, and startup costs you may face, make starting a marijuana business an expensive venture.

And once you are in business, the fees are high.

CHAPTER 7: HOW TO OBTAIN A LICENSE FOR A MEDICAL MARIJUANA DISPENSARY

Do you want to start a medical marijuana dispensary in the United States? If YES, here is a detailed guide on how to obtain a dispensary license in Texas, California, Florida, Michigan, Maryland. Marijuana is steadily gaining ground in the United States, although it still remains federally illegal. States have now begun to enact laws regulating the marijuana industry.

These laws determine who can grow or sell marijuana and under what conditions they can do so. Aside from medical and research purposes, most states have made the affairs of the marijuana dispensary legal. For this reason, many entrepreneurs are now considering owning marijuana dispensaries. To own and operate a marijuana dispensary in the US, you need to obtain a license. The type of license and documentation your marijuana company requires will depend on both the location of your operation and the type of business you are running.

This is why you need to do a lot of research before starting. If you are looking for ways to obtain a marijuana dispensary license in the United States, we have listed the states that have legalized marijuana dispensaries. We've also included where you can get these licenses and some of the guidelines you need to follow when applying.

A Detailed Guide to Obtaining a Marijuana Dispensing License in the United States Alaska.

It has been confirmed that Alaska is one of the states in the United States that allows the use of marijuana, but only for those 21 years of age and older.

This state authorizes companies to grow, produce and sell marijuana. If you want to open a marijuana dispensary in Alaska, you need to apply for a license, and this can be done online at the Department of Commerce, Community and Economic Development MARIJUANA ALCOHOL CONTROL OFFICE. Fingerprints must be submitted with each application. Fingerprint cards cannot be sent electronically to AMCO but physically. Applicants must use an approved agency to obtain their fingerprints. Marijuana growing permits, product manufacturing facilities, testing facilities, retail stores can also be obtained here.

Arizona

In Arizona, registered patients can possess and use medical marijuana. Licensed state-owned companies can grow, process, transport and distribute medical marijuana. All marijuana dispensary license applications must be filed online with the Arizona Department of Health Services. The site also lists the requirements for the application. Additionally, Arizona requires all cultivation facilities to be licensed as dispensaries. The Department will first determine if there is a county where there is no dispensary registration certificate. If there is one, then it would be easier to get a license there. All necessary information in this regard is available on the website.

Arkansas

Under Arkansas Dispensary Licenses, all individuals with legal prescription can possess and use medical marijuana. Licensed state-owned companies can grow, process, transport and distribute medical marijuana. The Arkansas Medical Marijuana Commission is responsible for the state's medical marijuana program. The commission had established strict guidelines for obtaining a dispensary license and they included: No more than 32 dispensary licenses will be awarded within the "8 dispensary zones".

Dispensary location cannot be less than 1,500 feet from a school, one church or kindergarten. No more than 1 license should be issued to any entity. The application fee for dispensary licenses is set at $ 7,500 (half of the application fee will be refunded if the license is not granted).

There is a two-tier licensing system for dispensaries: A tier of those dispensaries intending to grow marijuana will be included - a dispensary can choose to grow fifty (50) mature marijuana plants. A second tier will consist of those dispensaries that do not intend to grow marijuana. The applicant must declare their intention to grow or not to grow at the time of submitting the application. Within 7 days of receiving the commission's written notice of the selection, the selected applicant will be required to file a licensing fee of $ 15,000.00 in cash or certified funds, as well as a performance bond in the amount of $ 100,000.00.

California

In California, the Bureau issues temporary cannabis control marijuana dispensary licenses, cannabis growing licenses of CDFA, and cannabis safety branch produced by CDPH. Growers, producers, retailers, distributors, micro-enterprises, test labs and event organizers can apply for their licenses from these offices. Applications for annual licenses will be accepted through an online licensing system - the Manufactured Cannabis Licensing System (MLCS). This application will require information about the company, owners, financial interest holders and operating premises, as well as the description of procedures for waste disposal, inventory and quality control, transportation and safety. More information can be obtained on the California cannabis portal.

Colorado

If you intend to own a Colorado Retail Marijuana Business you should also visit the Colorado Marijuana Owners and Investors page. Licenses are available for both medical and recreational marijuana. The guidelines for obtaining a retail license in Colorado include that applicants; must apply to the state for a retail license before selling marijuana must confirm that the local authority in which they plan to operate allows retail marijuana stores to operate within their jurisdiction Applicants must be resident in the state of the Colorado for at least 2 years before applying for a license Number of retail stores licenses are limited by the local government Applicant must submit a non-refundable application fee of $ 4,500.

Connecticut

In Connecticut, all qualified patients with legal prescriptions can be in possession of marijuana, and licensed state companies can grow, process, transport, and dispense marijuana. The Connecticut Department of Consumer Protection is responsible for the States Medical Marijuana Program, and all applications are made there, by licensed manufacturers, patients, and qualified healthcare professionals. During application, there is a non-refundable application fee of $ 1,000 payable at the time of application and a non-refundable application fee of $ 5,000.

All marijuana businesses must be located at least 300 meters from places used primarily for religious worship, public or private school, convent, charitable institution, supported by public or private funds, hospital or veterans' home or from any military camp or establishment. Documentation that must be provided when submitting the application; Personal Information Latest Employment Information Dispensing Facility Information Licenses, Permits, and Records Professional History Criminal Actions Photo

Identification (Passport-sized Photograph and Copy of Valid Government-Issued ID) License Fee Initial Tuition Fee: $ 1,000 [non-refundable] Registration fee: $ 5,000 [non-refundable] Renewal fee: $ 5,000 [non-refundable] License and renewal fees: $ 100 each Registration / renewal of dispensary technician and dispensary staff: $ 50 Registration / Dispensary Facility Supporter Renewal: $ 100 Dispensary Name Change Application: $ 100 Dispensary Facility Manager Change: $ 50 Location Change or Expansion Application: $ 1,000 [plus $ 1,500 if approved] Application of physical, non-cosmetic modification of the structure [other than expansion]: $ 500 Questions and materials Support must be delivered by hand according to the instructions in the application request, along with an application fee of $ 25,000.

Delaware

In Delaware, anyone with a legal prescription can possess and use medical marijuana. Licensed state-owned companies can grow, process, transport and distribute medical marijuana. The Department of Health is responsible for issuing this license through the medical marijuana program. The state only grants licenses to compassion centers and has strict guidelines for opening these centers. They include; a compassion center must be run on a non-profit basis. A compassion center must not be located less than 300 meters from the property line of an existing public or private school. New applicants for a Compassion Center license will only be accepted during an open application period announced by the Department. A non-refundable application fee, made payable to the Division of Public Health, Medical Marijuana Program, in the amount of $ 5,000 will be required at the time of application. There is currently a compassion center and another opening soon.

Florida

Licensed distribution organizations are licensed to cultivate the process and dispense medical marijuana. These are the only companies in Florida licensed to distribute medical marijuana to qualified patients and legal representatives. The Office of Medical Marijuana Use (a division of the Florida Department of Health) is responsible for drafting and enforcing the department's rules and licensing activities for dispensing, processing and growing medical marijuana. The Office does not currently accept applications for medical marijuana treatment centers.

Hawaii

In Hawaii, anyone with a legal prescription can possess and use medical marijuana. Licensed state-owned companies can grow, process, transport and distribute medical marijuana. The Hawaii Department of Health Medical Cannabis Dispensing Program is responsible for licensing. The dispensary licensing guidelines for Hawaii are therefore; non-refundable application fee of $ 5,000. An application must state that applicants have resources in the amount of $ 1,000,000, plus a minimum of $ 100,000 for each retail location the applicant wishes to operate. A distributor licensee can manage up to two retail distribution points. If an applicant intends to operate two retail distribution points, the total money an applicant must have in reserve at the time of application is $ 1,200,000. Applicants can apply for more than one license, but only one license can be issued. If an applicant is entitled to more than one license, they will need to choose the county in which they want to operate a dispensary.

Illinois

In Illinois, all individuals with a legal prescription can possess and use medical marijuana. Licensed state-owned companies can grow, process, transport and distribute medical marijuana. The

Illinois Department of Financial and Professional Regulation is responsible for licensing dispensaries. At the moment they do not issue any licenses.

Iowa

In Iowa, qualified patients can use, possess and access low-THC cannabis oil. Cannabidiol production, delivery, transportation, and dispensing are permitted by authorized license holders. The Iowa Department of Public Health is authorized to select and license five medical cannabidiol dispensaries in Iowa. Dispensaries selected through the competitive process will obtain licenses from the department to legally provide medical cannabidiol to patients and primary caregivers with valid medical cannabidiol registration cards. Licensed dispensaries must be ready to begin providing medical cannabidiol by December 1, 2018. The law sets the non-refundable application fee for a dispensary license at $ 5,000. Louisiana In Louisiana, people with a legal recommendation from their doctor can be in possession of medical marijuana, and licensed state pharmacies can dispense medical marijuana. The Louisiana Board of Pharmacy is responsible for licensing. The state has a number of laws for opening dispensaries, and one of their laws limits the number of licenses to be distributed to 10.

Others include; Only existing pharmacies are allowed to dispense medical marijuana a single manufacturing facility will be responsible for growing, which one or both Louisiana State University and Southern University have the first right of refusal to grow medical marijuana collaboratively or separately. No more than 10 pharmacies can obtain licenses to dispense marijuana within the state. In the state, pharmacists can only dispense marijuana grown in state universities. Those wishing to prescribe medical marijuana in Louisiana must pay a $ 5,000 application fee in addition to a $ 150 licensing fee to become one of the 10 marijuana pharmacists in the state. The $ 5,000 application fee is non-refundable and only applies to marijuana pharmacies, not regular drug stores.

Main

In Maine, all individuals can be in possession of marijuana. The state is currently working on rules to establish a system for state-owned companies licensed to grow, process, transport and distribute recreational marijuana. License applicants must be at least 21 years old, citizens of Maine and have a verifiable SSN. Their businesses must be a corporation, association, corporation, corporation,

LLC or organization. If the applicant is a corporation, all board members must meet these criteria. Criminal convictions punishable by five years or more may automatically disqualify candidates, provided they have not elapsed 10 years or more since have occurred. Licenses for dispensaries are provided but are rarely available. The retail marijuana store license is as follows: license fee of $ 250- $ 2,500; non-refundable application fee of $ 10- $ 250

Maryland

In Maryland, all individuals with a prescription can possess and use medical marijuana. The Maryland Medical Cannabis Commission is responsible for developing policies, procedures and regulations for the use of medical marijuana, as well as licensing. It has issued medical cannabis dispensary pre - approvals to 102 companies, with 22 approved and the others in phase 2 of the approval process. Massachusetts In Massachusetts, people over the age of 21 can own up to one ounce of marijuana, keep up to 10 ounces of marijuana at home, and grow up to six plants.

Licensed state-owned enterprises can grow, produce, distribute and sell marijuana. All information on licensing marijuana establishments through the Cannabis Control Commission must be obtained on the Commission's website Applicants are required to pay $ 1,500 for the intent request and $ 30,000 for the management profile application and Operations Applications can be submitted by mail to the Cannabis Control Commission, 101 Federal Street, 13th Floor, Boston, MA 02110. In order to obtain a license in accordance with the Adult Marijuana Use Act passed in 2016, you need to apply for the Cannabis Control Commission.

Michigan

In Michigan, people 21 years of age and older can possess and use marijuana. Licensed state-owned companies can grow, process, transport and distribute marijuana. Here are some of the requirements to apply for a Michigan marijuana dispensary license; An applicant may have to pay a fee to their local city / municipality of up to $ 5000 and a non-refundable state application fee of $ 6000. The applicant, if an individual, must have been a resident of the State of Michigan for a continuous period of 2 years. This requirement does not apply after June 30, 2018. The applicant is ineligible if he has been convicted or released from incarceration under the laws of this state, any other state or United States (federal law) within the past 10 years or has been convicted of a controlled substance-related crime within the past 10 years.

The applicant is ineligible if he has been convicted of a crime involving a controlled substance, theft, dishonesty or fraud in any state within the past 5 years. Must apply for a procurement center license with the local city and state before selling marijuana and marijuana products. The Regulations of the Office of Medical Marijuana is responsible for the supervision of medical marijuana and is composed of the Medical Marijuana Program and the Facility Licensing Division. The Licensing and Regulatory Affairs Department is currently accepting applications for growers, processors, transporters, procurement centers and safety compliance facilities.

Minnesota

On May 29, 2014, Governor Mark Dayton signed a bipartisan medical marijuana proposal that was drafted by a House and Senate conference committee, making Minnesota the 22nd state to exempt some sufferers and their caregivers from penalty for using marijuana with a medical certification. Licenses for marijuana companies are not available. The Department of Health has selected two companies as registered marijuana producers and distributors. The state has 8 dispensaries, which are called centers for cannabis patients.

A non-refundable application fee of $ 20,000 is required for registration. Montana In Montana, only registered cardholders are allowed to own and use marijuana. The Montana Department of Public Health and Human Services is in charge of the States Medical Marijuana Program. Questions for the provider, test lab, and dispensary licenses are available periodically. The proposed test rooms or laboratories may not be less than 150 meters away and on the same street as a building used exclusively as a church, synagogue or other place of worship or secondary school or post-school other than a commercially operated school.

Nevada

Nevada legalized medical marijuana on November 7, 2000, when 65% of the population voted yes on question 9. The Nevada Tax Department is responsible for licensing and regulating retail marijuana businesses and the program state medical marijuana. As of November 2018, only holders of existing medical marijuana establishment certificates can apply for a retail marijuana establishment license.

Fees you may incur in attempting to open a dispensary in Nevada Medical Marijuana Institution Registration Certificate: $ 5,000 [non-refundable, applies to all of the following in addition to lower fees] Pantry Registration Certificate: $ 30,000 Pantry Certificate Renewal: $ 5,000 Growing Facility Registration Certificate: $ 3,000 Growing Facility Certificate Renewal: $ 1,000 Facility producing edible marijuana or marijuana products - Certificate of Registration: $ 3,000 Edible Manufacturing Facility Certificate Renewal: $ 1,000 MM Agent Registration Card: $ 75 Card Renewal Agent: $ 75 Certificate of Registration of independent testing laboratory: $ 5,000 Renewal of certain Independent Testing Lab Fee: $ 3,000 Some guidelines include that applicants must submit a non-refundable application fee of $ 5,000.

They must show proof of the amount of taxes paid or other beneficial financial contributions paid to this State or its political subdivisions over the past 5 years by the applicant or persons who purport to be owners, officers or board members of the proposal marijuana plant.

Again, the retail marijuana store must be at least 300m from a public or private school and 30m from a community facility. Not more than 80 licenses issued in a county with a population of less than 700,000. No more than 20 licenses issued in a county with a population of less than 700,000 but more than 100,000. Note more than 4 licenses issued in a county with a population of less than 100,000 but greater than 55,000. No more than 2 licenses issued in a county with a population of less than 55,000.

New Hampshire

In New Hampshire, anyone with a legal prescription can possess and use medical marijuana. The New Hampshire Department of Health and Human Services is responsible for managing the cannabis therapeutic program. The Department established the New Hampshires term for 4 Alternative Treatment Center (ATC) dispensaries. These centers are the only ones needed to own, grow, acquire, deliver, produce, transfer, supply, sell, distribute and transport cannabis and other related supplies, as well as educational materials for both eligible patients and other alternative treatment centers.

New Jersey

In New Jersey, all people with a legal prescription can be in possession of marijuana, and licensed state companies can grow, process, transport and dispense marijuana. The New Jersey Department of Health is in charge of the States Medicinal Marijuana Program. State licensing firms called Alternative Treatment Centers (ATCs) for the production and distribution of medical marijuana. Six ATCs have been licensed. Once the initial six are opened, the state will evaluate the program and determine whether or not expansion is needed. At present, however, the state does not license any medical marijuana business.

New Mexico

The New Mexico Department of Health is responsible for overseeing the medical cannabis program. To produce, distribute and distribute medical marijuana, you must be a licensed nonprofit producer (LNPP). A nonprofit producer operates a facility and, at any one time, is limited to a combined total of no more than 450 mature female male plants, seedlings, and plants. The period LNPP application is closed and the department is not currently accepting applications for the medical marijuana production and distribution. Currently, there are 50 licensed cannabis dispensaries in New Mexico with an estimated 50,954 registered patients. At the end of 2016, the size of the cannabis market in New Mexico exceeded $ 50.6 million.

New York

The New York Department of Health is in charge of its medical marijuana program. Only registered organizations can produce and distribute medical marijuana. The Department began accepting applications for registration as a registered organization on April 27, 2015. Each applicant was required to submit two fees with their application: a non-refundable application fee in the amount of $ 10,000 and a registration fee for an amount of $ 200,000. The $ 200,000 registration fee is to be refunded to the applicant only if the applicant has not been issued a registration. The Department does not currently accept applications to become a registered organization.

North Dakota

The Division of Medical Marijuana (part of the North Dakota Department of Health) is in charge of the state's medical marijuana program. Compassion centers are dispensaries or facilities for marijuana growers / producers. The application period for compassion centers is currently closed. Some of their application guidelines include that: Compassion centers are required to maintain adequate security, including well-lit entrances, an alarm system that contacts law enforcement, and video surveillance. They may not be within 1,000 feet of a school and will be subject to inspections and other regulations. There is a $ 5,000 non-refundable application fee to submit a proposal (application) and a $ 90,000 certification fee upon issuance of the license. Compassion Center licenses will be granted on the basis of a merit-based application procedure, which will consider: the suitability of the proposed venue; the character and competence of applicants in related fields; proposed center plans, including those related to record keeping, security, personnel and training, to prevent diversion. Every staff member of a compassion center must apply for and obtain a registry photo ID card. They must be at least 21 years of age and must not have been convicted of a crime of barred crime or a recent drug. Compassion Center membership fee is non-refundable.

Ohio

Under new regulations, enacted on September 8, 2016, Ohio is ready to welcome medical marijuana businesses. While the state has already licensed a limited number of growers, dispensaries, and other businesses, it can issue multiple licenses as needed to meet demand.

Oklahoma

With the death of SQ 788 in June 2018, Oklahoma became the 30th state in the United States to legalize medical marijuana. Oklahoma residents over the age of 18 with a valid medical recommendation can apply for a license for a medical marijuana patient. If approved, they can purchase medical marijuana from licensed dispensaries across the state. Dispensaries in Oklahoma must be located at least 300 meters from a public or private school. This is measured by a straight line (the shortest distance) from the dispensary property line to any school entrance. The Oklahoma State Department of Health is responsible for approving licenses and they have some application criteria which include; The applicant must be twenty five (25) years of age or older; Any applicant, presenting himself as an individual, must exhibit residence in the state of Oklahoma; All applying entities must demonstrate that all members, officers and board members are resident in Oklahoma; An applicant entity can show ownership of non-Oklahoma residents, but this percentage cannot exceed 25%. All applicant persons or entities must be registered to conduct business in the state of Oklahoma; All applicants must disclose all ownership; Applicant (s) with only convictions for nonviolent crimes in the past two (2) years, any other felony convictions over five (5) years, convicts or any other person currently incarcerated are not eligible for a medical marijuana dispensary license.

Oregon

In 2013, Oregon House Bill 3460 became law, allowing medical marijuana dispensaries to be registered. The legislation went into effect on March 1, 2014. Licenses are mandatory and available for medical and recreational marijuana companies. The state requires separate licenses and registrations for growers and dispensary operators. The Oregon Liquor Control Commission (OLCC) license accepts applications for marijuana licenses. The application fee is usually $ 3,500 and the application fee is $ 500. There is also an annual tracking system fee of $ 480. Each applicant must also pay $ 35 for a background check. Furthermore, there will be a huge capital of up to $ 500,000 to open a new cannabis dispensary.

Rhode Island

According to state law of Rhode Island, cannabis businesses such as dispensaries, must be defined as compassion centers. A compassion center in the state of Rhode Island can do any of the following: growing, processing, transporting, as well as selling cannabis to all registered patients and registered primary care providers. Applications can only be submitted during an open application period announced by the state if necessary. The state has 3 licensed compassion centers currently in operation. Each application for a compassion center must include: A non-refundable application fee paid to the department in the amount of two hundred and fifty dollars ($ 250); The proposed law name and proposed incorporation of the compassion center; the proposed physical address of the compassion center, if a specific address has been determined or, if not, the general location where it would be located. This may include a second location for medical marijuana cultivation; A description of the closed and closed facility that would be used in the cultivation of marijuana; The name, address, and date of birth of each principal officer and board member of the compassion center; Proposed safety and security measures that include at least one security alert system for each location, planned measures to deter and prevent unauthorized entry into areas containing marijuana and theft of marijuana, as well as a draft, instruction manual for employees which includes security policies, personal safety and security procedures, and crime prevention techniques; and Proposed procedures to ensure accurate record keeping.

Tennessee

In 2014 the state approved SB 2531, a limited medical bill for cannabis, which permits the use of cannabis oil containing CBAAD as part of the Aa clinical research study on its effects on patients with seizure disorders. Tennessee Tech has the opportunity to grow, process and distribute CBD. In Tennessee, qualified patients can own and use CBD extracts. Current law does not provide for a state-regulated dispensary system. Texas In Texas, only clinically qualified people are allowed to own or use CBD oil. Licensed state-owned companies can brew, grow and process low-THC marijuana. The Texas Department of Public Safety (DPS) issues the license. The license will authorize organizations to cultivate the process and dispense low-THC cannabis to prescribed patients. The department under the state bill is required to license only three donor organizations, and these organizations have already been licensed. For now, the state is not receiving applications.

Utah

In Utah, qualified registered patients can possess and use medical marijuana. Authorized state agencies can grow, process and distribute medical marijuana. The Utah Department of Health is responsible for licensing applicants. The applicant will need an operational plan that includes operating procedures that comply with the law; Including financial statements showing that the applicant has a minimum of $ 500,000 in liquid assets available to each cannabis growing facility for which the person applies, or a minimum of $ 100,000 in liquid assets available to each processing facility. cannabis or independent cannabis testing laboratory for which the person applies. Vermont The Department of Public Safety is responsible for the marijuana registry and issues dispensary registration certificates. The Department has issued 4 dispensary registration certificates and 1 conditional certificate. The Department plans to announce an application period for a sixth dispensary once the number of registered patients reaches 7,000. Currently, dispensaries are the only types of licensed marijuana companies in Vermont. Licensees can operate two dispensaries with the same permit. It is advisable to understand state regulations and also to treat the marijuana business in line with local laws. Application fees are as follows: $ 2,500 for the dispensary application $ 50 for the caregiver enrollment application License fees include: $ 20,000 Initial Waiver Registration Fee $ 25,000 Renewal Waiver Registration Fee.

Washington

In 2012, Washington became the first US state to legalize the recreational use of cannabis after more than a decade of medical legalization. With the demise of Initiative 502, adults over the age of 21 were legally allowed to purchase and own cannabis products from licensed distributors. The Washington State Liquor and Cannabis Board is responsible for licensing marijuana; however, it does not currently accept license requests. Washington DC While it is legal to use marijuana recreationally, there are no businesses that sell marijuana for recreational use. The DC Department of Health has a medical marijuana program, but does not currently accept applications for medical marijuana facilities.

Wisconsin

In Wisconsin, qualified patients can own and use CBD extracts. State-licensed doctors and pharmacies can dispense CBD extracts to patients. The state of Wisconsin does not currently accept applications for marijuana companies. West Virginia Governor Jim Justice signed Senate Bill 386, known as the Medical Cannabis Act, on April 20, 2017, making medical marijuana use legal for qualified patients in West Virginia. Patients will be able to obtain medical cannabis in the following forms: pill, oil, topical forms including gels, creams or ointments, a medically appropriate form for administration by vaporization or nebulization, tincture, liquid or dermal patch. The state intends to issue around 30 dispensary permits to individuals. Individuals wishing to obtain a West Virginia dispensing permit must submit an application that includes the following: Verification of all principals, operators, financiers or employees of a medical cannabis grower / processor or distributor. A description of your responsibilities as a principal, operator, financier or employee. Any releases required to obtain information from government agencies, employers and other organizations. A criminal background checks. Details of any licenses, permits or other similar authorizations obtained in another jurisdiction, including any suspension, revocation or regulation in that jurisdiction. A description of the commercial activities in which it intends to engage as a medical cannabis organization The application for a license permit will require specific business plans A statement that the applicant: has a good moral character. Possesses the ability to quickly obtain the right to use sufficient land, buildings and other premises and equipment to properly carry out the activity described in the application and any proposed location for a facility. is able to maintain effective security and control to prevent diversion, abuse and other illegal conduct related to medical cannabis. Is able to comply with all applicable state laws and regulations relating to the activities in which the applicant intends to engage under this act. Name, residential address and title of each lender and principal of the applicant. Any other information requested by the Office of Public Health States without laws on the use of marijuana for medical or recreational use.

States that currently prohibit the use of marijuana or severely limit its use include: Alabama, Georgia, Idaho, Indiana, Kansas, Kentucky, Mississippi, Nebraska, New Hampshire, North Carolina, South Carolina, South Dakota, and Wyoming.

CHAPTER 8: LICENSES IN THE REST OF THE WORLD

Canada officially passed the C-45 (Cannabis Act) in October 2018, making it the only G7 country that allows the cultivation and sale of recreational cannabis. This means that cannabis in Canada is federally legal. All aspects of the sale and distribution of cannabis are however under provincial jurisdiction, with different rules for licensing retailers. The Cannabis Legalization and Regulation Branch (CLRB) is responsible for overseeing the licensing process.

Where and how the license is obtained in Canada depends on the province that will host the office. For example, in British Columbia it is necessary to obtain a license as a private enterprise from the British Columbia Liquor and Cannabis Regulation Branch (LCRB) following a detailed application procedure. In Manitoba, the Manitoba Liquor and Gaming Authority (LGA) issues retail licenses, but individual municipalities can veto the opening of stores in their area.

In Ontario, a license as a dispensary can be obtained by following a detailed application process to be sent to Ontario Cannabis Retail

Corporation (OCRC). In Alberta, the application is sent to the Alberta Gaming and Liquor Commission (AGLC).

EUROPE

Unlike Canada and the United States where cannabis is legal, all EU Member States consider possessing cannabis for personal use a criminal offense. However, several countries such as Spain, Italy, the Czech Republic and Belgium have begun to eliminate imprisonment as a penalty for minor offenses.

No government in Europe openly supports the legalization of cannabis for recreational use: the legal cannabis market in Europe exists today only in a medical context. Even dispensaries and coffeeshops in the Netherlands are simply tolerated as long as they follow strict criteria set by the public authority. It works in a similar way to cannabis clubs in Spain, which are technically private places, not retail commercial spaces.

Due to the legal status of cannabis in European nations, it is not yet possible to apply for a license to sell recreational cannabis today, although small steps have been taken.

Germany, for example, awarded the first national licenses for growing medical cannabis in 2019, although the process has so far been complicated by setbacks and delays. Germany recently restarted the application process and companies that will be selected to legally grow German medical cannabis will have to comply with strict safety requirements and the highest pharmaceutical manufacturing standards.

How to Open A Social Club

Cannabis Social Club: how one works and how to open one

Cannabis Social Clubs are to all intents and purposes non-profit associations duly constituted, with a Statute, an internal organization and maximum openness to dialogue with the Authorities, which intend to develop in countries where the personal consumption of cannabis is decriminalized, with the aim of being able to practice collective cultivation and satisfy - in a legal and non-profit manner - the personal consumption of adult members who are part of it, thus establishing a closed circuit between growers and consumers, where the entire process of production, distribution and consumption is subject to the supervision of the Authorities and, above all, is free from illicit drug trafficking and any other illegal activity on which the greatest risks for consumers depend, including as regards abuse and problematic use cannabis and other substances.

Starting a Cannabis Social Club in 4 steps

According to Article 12 of the Charter of Fundamental Rights of the European Union: "everyone has the right to freedom of peaceful assembly and association at all levels" and, as long as their activities do not threaten health and / or order public, the Authorities have no reason to interfere.

Wanting to hypothesize the establishment of a Cannabis Social Club, it is essential to avoid any connection with the black market, because a CSC that can be defined as such, not only must seem legal, but must also be really so, in order to be able to prove it during a any trial at your own expense. Therefore, it is good to never forget that the organization and management of a CSC requires a lot of seriousness and strict discipline.

To function, every Cannabis Social Club needs members who actively participate in the organization and management, in various forms and with different responsibilities.

The rules of conduct within the CSC must be clear and simple, respected and controlled in a democratic way. From the outset, it is advisable to seek legal assistance from a lawyer who can offer advice on the steps to be taken before, during and after the start of the CSC, as well as preparing a legal defense line in the event that it becomes necessary.
Furthermore, even before considering the idea of starting a Cannabis Social Club, it is good to check the legal framework regarding the consumption of Cannabis in force in your country: if it is not considered a criminally punishable crime, the personal possession of which, within certain limits, it is sanctioned "only" administratively (as is the case in Italy), in theory it should be possible to organize an adequate legal defense of the Cannabis Social Club.

Phase 1: public presentation of the initiative

The first step towards starting a Cannabis Social Club is the presentation of your initiative through a press conference and / or the public dissemination of the news (social network, website, magazine, newspapers and local TV, etc...). The best way to do this is by trying to involve a well-known personality (politicians, artists, sportsmen, etc...), in order to benefit from adequate visibility and to reduce as much as possible the possibility of being prosecuted for possession - always within the limits of personal consumption - of seeds, plants or quantities of cannabis during the presentation phases of your initiative.

Furthermore, again in the context of this presentation, it is very important to underline (in the clearest and most incisive way possible) how the sole purpose of the Cannabis Social Club is to undertake the cultivation conduct for the exclusive personal consumption of the adult members of the CSC and to offer a legal, safe and transparent alternative to illicit drug trafficking.

If there is no reaction on the part of the legal activities that could suggest the intent to pursue the initiative, it is possible to move on to "phase 2".

Phase 2: establishment of the Cannabis Social Club

The next phase is the official constitution of the Cannabis Social Club: a non- profit association, made up of cannabis consumers (EXCLUSIVELY ADULTS) of Cannabis, who collectively grow, through a closed circuit, the quantity necessary for their personal consumption.

It is necessary to create an executive committee that includes at least the figures of the President, the secretary and the treasurer and establish a democratic and transparent decision-making process, so that all club members can be aware of the main steps of the organization, the adoption of financial agreements, etc.

The statute must necessarily contain the purpose of the association: to reduce and avoid the health risks that could derive from the irresponsible use and / or abuse of Cannabis, as well as to reduce and avoid the risks associated with sourcing on the black market, in legal and health terms (adulteration of cannabis, incitement to the use of hard drugs, etc.). The objectives can also be related to the study of the plant for research purposes, the use of cultivation methods that exclusively respect the standards of organic farming and the promotion of a social debate on the legal status of Cannabis and on the requalification of consumers.

The statute of a Cannabis Social Club, like that of any other non-profit association, should be duly registered and legally recognized by the competent authorities.

To get started, users need to be allowed to join the club (making sure they are adults who are already cannabis users and / or have a recognized medical condition that cannabis use cannot be harmful, if not therapeutic).

At this point, cultivation begins! It is necessary to establish a priori the quantity of plants necessary for the personal consumption of the members and to organize collective production in a common plantation. Cultivation should be exclusively organic and ensure an adequate variety of plants available, so that club members can continuously experiment with new cannabis species and identify the ones that best suit their needs.

Make sure that the people who conduct the cultivation and possibly carry out the transport of plants, inflorescences and / or other ready-to-use derivatives are always in possession of the documentation that specifies the activity of the association and that refers to the legal antecedents. The documentation should be such as to show that the cannabis in the collective plantation was grown in the name of the club members, identifiable in an official registry (for example a card containing a copy of the identity documents). This documentation could be crucial to avoid the prosecution of the people involved in the association, in the event that the judicial authority could decide to intervene.

Whether the distribution and consumption of cannabis can take place within the club, it all depends on the legislation in your country and on the correct interpretation in case of trial.

Phase 3: Make your club more professional

Over time, the number of club members will grow and the organization of production, transportation, payments, etc. will need to become more professional. In order to allow the association to manage the cultivation well, it is advisable to set up several small-scale plantations.

Each club can have its own rules, which integrate and extend those on the statute, to regulate the use of the environments available to members to consume their cannabis, the methods of payment of the membership fee, the cultivation methods, the good spirit of the group, etc. In these rules it is possible to include the code of conduct for members, for example the absolute ban on selling Cannabis produced to non members, even more so if to minors.

CHAPTER 9: LICENSES AND BUREAUCRATIC PROCEDURES IN THE USA

Eleven states in the United States have so far legalized cannabis for non-medical use by adults, with many more ready to follow. With cannabis still federally illegal, a number of natural experiments are underway, each presenting a different model of how cannabis can be regulated, thus providing important lessons to policymakers seeking to pursue similar policies. In this report, we compare regulation between states, taking into account key objectives, including public health and social justice, and consider the lessons that can be learned for future policy reform.

The transition from the market to therapeutic use

Cannabis is now legal for medical purposes in most of the United States, so many states have drawn the architecture of their non-medical cannabis distribution system on existing models. Illinois, for example, implemented an "early demand" system for companies already licensed to retail medical cannabis in the area before sales began in January 2020. In Michigan, the Marijuana Regulatory Agency has made it mandatory to have a state operating license for medical cannabis.

While such strategies simplify the administrative process of developing a new retail market, they also create significant barriers to entry, particularly for small businesses and suppliers based in local communities. Therefore, the current medical cannabis production and sales infrastructure does not offer the best platform for non-medical procurement if the goal is to promote local involvement. The investment necessary to start structures oriented to medical production inevitably excludes small producers, even if giving priority to activities in the therapeutic field allows for an easier regulatory transition.

Licensing

Licensing is the key mechanism for regulating sales and controlling product availability. States have adopted a number of different licensing systems, leading to different results.

Cannabis license in the United States

All states have tried to give municipalities and local authorities some degree of autonomy in regulating non-medicinal cannabis within their communities: including the flexibility of zoning rules or the option to ban retailers altogether. In California, this has led to 76% of cities rejecting cannabis shops, leading to criticism that the patchwork of bans is undermining regulatory efforts to tackle the illegal market at the state level. States seek a balance in ensuring access to retail markets taking into account the concerns of municipalities and have responded in several ways. In Oregon, for example, cities and counties had direct authority until December 2015 to enforce local bans if their residents voted at least 55% against legalization, although only five cities did.

Taxation

Legal regulation allows you to tax profits from cannabis markets. The income tax can be spent in various ways in addition to financing the implementation of the regulatory framework, including social projects (if desired). However, it is also a key lever for influencing the retail price.

Some states have tried to allocate revenue (or "mortgage" it) for social purposes. In Illinois, 20% of state cannabis taxes go to basic services to "tackle substance abuse... prevention and mental health problems" and 2% go to the Drug Treatment Fund to help with its campaign of public education and, consequently, analyze the public health impacts of regulation. In Oregon, 20% of the taxes go directly to the Mental Health Alcoholism and Drug Services Account which provides assistance for the prevention, intervention and treatment of drug abuse and an additional 5% goes to the health authority for the prevention and alcohol and drug abuse.

State Excise and Other taxes

Washington 37%, 7-10% additional state and local sales tax.

Colorado 15%, additional 15% "special marijuana sales tax" and additional 2.9% state sales tax.

Illinois 10% for THC <35%

25% for THC> 35%

20% on all cannabis infusions

Additional 7% cultivation tax on gross income.

Municipalities and counties can add additional taxes to stores of up to 3% and 3.75%.

Nevada 15% of the wholesale price (paid by the grower)
10% on retail
Retail sales tax at the local rate.

Oregon 17%. Up to 3% additional local taxes.

Massachusetts 10.75%. Additional state sales tax of 6.25% and optional local tax up to 3%.

Maine 10%. Additional 10% sales tax on grower-to-retailer or derivatives producers' sales.

California 15%. Growth Fee Per Ounce of Dry Goods: $ 9.25 for flowers; $ 2.75 for the leaves or $ 1.29 for the cannabis plant.

Local governments may apply additional taxes.

Michigan 10%. Additional 6% state sales tax.

Alaskan Sprouts and Ripe Flowers: $ 50 an ounce ; $ 15 per ounce.

Abnormal / immature buds and flowers: $ 25 an ounce.

Cuttings: $ 1 for cuttings.

Vermont N / A

Packaging, advertising and marketing

All states have packaging controls, including defining various "universal symbology" systems to ensure it is clear when a product contains cannabis, as well as including warnings about potential driving hazards or the need to stay out of the reach of children. In some states there are specific restrictions to prevent accidental use by children, which include a ban on using characters that children like, such as cartoon characters.

All states require the THC content to be specified on the package. All states also require that cannabis be contained in resealable and child-resistant packages and in all states, except Oregon, they must be opaque. The degree of uniformity on this issue reflects a certain consensus on the common goals of regulation, especially in relation to public health and the protection of minors.

Removal from the criminal record (definitive cancellation)

The moves to regulate this product represent a radical change in social views on cannabis use; however, criminal records remain an enduring stigma that people carry with them. The so-called "permanent deletion", which means the destruction or deletion of an individual from the criminal record, allows states to remove this burden from individuals and, to some extent, recognize the errors of previous policy. Annulment is technically different from the "Record Seal", a process whereby the precedent in the criminal record is not deleted, but hidden from the public register and therefore can only be recalled in certain situations.

Status Type of removal of the previous penalty

California Record Seal Yes

Oregon Sealing Record
Individuals can file a motion to request a court order to overturn convictions for DST conduct. A law in 2020 removed the demand for payment of taxes.

Nevada Seal Record
Individuals can apply for a court order to overturn convictions for now decriminalized conduct.

Vermont Expungement / Seal Record
Individuals can file a petition requesting deletion or sealing from the criminal record if the conduct is no longer prohibited by law or defined as a crime.

Washington Sealing Record
The individual can submit a request to the court to overturn convictions for minor cannabis-related offenses. An expedited pardon from the governor is also possible.

Washington State law does not allow for permanent cancellation.

Record seal of Colorado
At the state level, only record sealing is allowed, but in Dever and Boulder, minor offenses related to cannabis no longer punishable (such as possessing less than an ounce of cannabis) can be overruled.

Massachusetts Expungement
The court can order the cancellation of a "crime at registration which at the time of cancellation is no

longer a crime", but an individual petition is required.

Illinois Expungement

The penal system is obliged to automatically delete any annotation no longer condemned by certain dates. The Governor can grant a pardon by authorizing the cancellation of penalties for possession, production and possession with the aim of selling up to 30 grams of cannabis. For larger quantities, the subject can file an application for cancellation to the State Prosecutor (up to 500gr).

Maine. A law has been proposed that would oblige "the Department of Public Security to cancel, by 1 July 2020, all criminal records relating to conduct offenses now authorized by the legislation on the use of marijuana for adults". But the bill was later declared "dead".

The removal of criminal records can be complicated, and administrative and economic barriers can prevent people from clearing their criminal records, even if it is technically possible. One way to solve this problem is to automate the elements of the process. In California, Bill 1793 requires the Justice Department to review past convictions relating to cannabis to determine all cases that qualify for the withdrawal or revocation of a sentence, revocation and "sealing" or redefinition, by July 1. 2020. In this case the minutes of the seal are effective and automatic: the execution is the sole responsibility of the Department of Justice, rather than forcing the parties concerned to submit their requests.

Social equity measures
Legal regulation of cannabis supply gives states the opportunity to repair damage to individuals and communities disproportionately affected by the cannabis ban. Legal cannabis is a potentially lucrative industry, and proactive measures are needed to ensure that the benefits are not only widely shared, but directed at the communities that have suffered the most from the ban. In some (but not all) states, social equity measures have become a key feature of cannabis regulation to ensure market access for disproportionately affected groups.

As companies need a license to produce or sell cannabis, social equity measures can be integrated into license application procedures to promote access for those affected disproportionately. In Nevada, "corporate diversity" (meaning the presence, in the company, of people of different ethnicity, culture, society, age and gender) is required and counted when license applications are evaluated and ends up in the overall scores of candidates in Illinois. Up to one fifth of the points in the dispensary's license application scoring system are eligible for social equity applicant status. Additional measures to facilitate market access include exemptions and loans. Illinois has proposed a low-interest lending program in areas where the ban has had a disproportionate impact, with funding of $ 30 million, as well as tax cuts of up to 50%. Loan programs also help mitigate financial barriers to startups. This is particularly important since the lack of banking services available to cannabis companies (since the banks are banned from having relationships with companies "illegal" at the federal level) was reported as an "effective blockade for almost all" if not rich and well connected, from entering and benefiting from the industry ". While loans and tax exemptions are key to promoting early access to the industry, training, technical assistance and mentoring, such as those offered by the Massachusetts Social Equity Program, are key to ensuring long-term success.

Conversely, some states have no social equity schemes at all. Washington state, for example, has been criticized for failing to support minority groups in the cannabis industry. In response, it detailed new proposals to increase corporate diversity, but it's unclear how practical they are, especially as they aren't currently accepting new license applications. The difficulty of applying equity measures retrospectively highlights the critical importance of putting diversity and corporate equity at the heart of the regulatory framework from the outset.

Lessons learned

The legal regulation of cannabis is still relatively new. We cannot know the full impact until policies have had time to roll out and long-term market readjustments have taken place. In the United States we are seeing a number of approaches, with large differences between states but also a high level of "policy transfer". It is unclear how these approaches will shape the size and pattern of markets in the long term; however, we can already begin to see how different regulatory models lead or facilitate different outcomes. For example, the direct shift of the system from medical to non-medical retail may exclude smaller operators; allowing the possibility of a local ban, while creating local democratic accountability, can also create a regulatory mosaic; the availability of "permanent deletion" processes can be compromised if these are overly complicated; and failing to establish proactive measures of social equity from the start can reinforce inequality in the new market and create an environment in which those most affected by the previous system are excluded from reaping the benefits of change.

The United States is undergoing a revolution in their approach to cannabis. Like all revolutions, however, the results are uncertain. Legal regulation offers a unique opportunity to address the dire injustices that prevent normalization, but it can also transfer financial benefits away from local communities and into the pockets of large corporations. Regulation should not replace one set of inequalities with others. Looking through the experiences of states that have legalized so far, we can see the drift in both directions: corporate dominance and a lack of market access to groups that have been disproportionately affected by the ban in some cases, careful efforts to ensure the economic inclusion and addressing historical injustice in others. Getting the best results is often a matter of detail: How are licensing systems built in relation to entry costs? What are the systems for managing past convictions? What are the precise rules on marketing and promotion? As we move through high-level debates for change in a world where it is already happening, these details matter. Therefore, while we are still awaiting evidence of some long-term consequences, this report suggests that there are essential considerations that must be part of the regulatory design from the start if the goals are to be achieved: improving public health, protecting health, human rights and the promotion of social justice in the best possible way.

CHAPTER 10: HOW MUCH DOES IT COST TO OPEN A DISPENSARY?

Opening a Cannabis Dispensary in Illinois will be expensive due to the costs of security, capital requirements, licensing, consulting, and legal costs, which continue in your company's operations.

Get ready and build a great team and business plan and get the right consultants and resources for your success.

The experts we spoke to believe that the costs of opening your cannabis business in Illinois will range from $ 400,000 to $ 1,000,000 for a dispensary and from $ 6.5 million to $ 10 million for artisanal grows, depending on the location and size of buildings.

Each state is a little different, but if you want to open a dispensary or grow in Illinois, the regulations and limited number of licenses increase the cost more than in non-competitive states.

Here is a quick rundown of the start-up costs to open a handcrafted cannabis dispensary in Illinois:

Statutory commissions

Costs of compiling the application

Legal fees

Cannabis Operations Consultant Fees

Fees for accountants and other professionals

Insurance premiums

Community outreach costs

Properly capitalized requirements

Construction of buildings and fixed rental costs

Employees

Costs of flowers and inventory

Renewal license fees

Taxes (IRC 280E)

Marketing

Professional commissions in progress

These are the simplest costs: the taxes you pay to the state of Illinois. They are provided for by statute and have a number. Simple to plug into your budget, but that's just the tip-to-toe cost of your cannabis companies to open their dispensary or grow artisanally.

For dispensaries:
Non-refundable application fee of $ 5,000.
$ 60,000 registration fee (renewable for the same amount every two years.)

For Craft Grows:
Non-refundable application fee of $ 5,000.
$ 40,000 application fee (becomes a renewable fee)

Start-up costs and location of your cannabis dispensary
Real estate is all about location, so where you open your cannabis business is important. Rent, as the cannabis business cannot cash in on a real estate mortgage, is the main driver of a large budget for your cannabis business.

Cannabis real estate is often referred to as a "green zone"

Your dispensary square footage will impact your double taxation under IRC 280E and also your rental costs. Although growers are not impressed with IRC 280E, they must maintain buildings within closed loop system if they are to maintain the highest quality product.

You have to plan and imagine your cannabis business very precisely, with the help of talented designers and architects, to determine not only your startup needs, but also your daily operating costs.

How much does it cost to open a dispensary as a tenant?

Expect a market rent premium and possible zoning problems. Fortunately, dispensaries in Illinois have six months from the granting of their conditional use dispensing license to provide the state with its address.

Also, security issues related to the location of your property should be explored and discussed in your plan because security is an important point. The same goes for the build outs and security features needed to be integrated into your craft dispensing or growing business, which aren't as stringent in the West Coast states.

The costs of furniture, fixtures and equipment (FF&E) in Illinois are higher due to the level of security built into the law to prevent the diversion of cannabis from the supply chain or the robberies of money that only adults use in cannabis.

The consultants will help you put together your cannabis license application, business plan, financial plans, security plans, social equity plans, and numerous other things. The completed question will resemble what in the 20th century was known as a "rubric". The phrase means that a high-scoring application's stack of papers will be large, perhaps hundreds of pages.

The reason for the length of the application has to do with the promises your cannabis company is making to the state of Illinois (and to your state if you are somewhere else) about its application.

After you are granted a license to grow or distribute cannabis to your business, all the terms and conditions and promises regarding your cannabis business that you have made in the application actually become requirements to run your business!

Your application requires employee training policies, public awareness plans, security design and protocols, sophisticated business operations, financial and property contracts, and the important record keeping systems and procedures employed in growing or selling cannabis for adult use.

No other company has so much advance planning that it is licensed to open its doors.

If you've ever heard an entrepreneur complain about overly burdensome regulations, ask if they're in the cannabis industry.
The application process can cost tens of thousands of dollars and will be described more fully below. The important thing your business can do when taking the risk of applying for its license is to purchase at least one good application.
Illinois has very few places open for the first wave of the industry. Maybe you'll do the first wave, or the second or the third.

A cannabis business plan (team) can control startup costs

When drafting your business plan, use this team mindset when combining: your culture, your key legal, tax, security and operational advisors, your investors and, of course, your clients.

Illinois adds a new wrinkle to the traditional cannabis business plans of other adult consumption states: social equity. You can use social equity goals to open up the cannabis industry to those who have been most influenced by drug laws over the past 80 years. Perhaps your cannabis company will come up with a plan to hire 10 full-time candidates for social equity so that your company can be proudly recognized for helping meet the state's goals in its new adult use law.

Obviously, the business plan should have traditional revenue and expense projections and an experienced financial planner or CPA with previous retail experience, (and hopefully cannabis experience) will get your business the most reliable figures. Cannabis business plans, unlike simple business plans, often have to address business aspects resulting from regulatory compliance.

For example, you will have to bear compliance costs to ensure that your operation complies with new and evolving laws in its operations and how they can be addressed by software or human resources.

Our cannabis lawyers think it is a good rule of thumb to observe how the state is evaluating applications for cannabis dispensary or craft grow licenses and speak directly to each aspect when you answer all the elements required by the application, with detailed plans and descriptions of why your company is the right candidate for the job as a licensed cannabis grower or craft dispensary.

Safety plan for the distribution of cannabis or artisanal cultivation

Safety doesn't just mean having a tough guy with a gun. Security combines technology, structural design and law enforcement surveillance best practices to implement a system that, if something goes wrong, who did it, when it was done, and what exactly happened, is captured in high definition, printed and provided appropriately to the law enforcement authorities.

Security is also built into your property in its layout, customer experience stream, doors, cameras, building materials, and even employee training policies and procedures. The security plan aspect of your application counts for many points. Cannabis businesses cost a lot to open, but the initial cost is to fill out the right safety plan so that it meets your state approval and gets a high score.

Record-keeping plan to prevent cannabis diversion or cash costs

Many companies have proprietary software that was invented before Illinois even became a medical cannabis state. These are the ancillary activities that arise when cannabis becomes a legal activity. The software you will use to track product supply and sales will depend on the consultant you choose. You don't want your Point of Sale (POS) system to be a real, well, POS.

If your cannabis business plan includes developing such technologies in its five-year plans to create additional income streams by selling licenses for what it builds, employee training plans and policies should also have best practices in place providing an accurate record. These procedures must be followed and include training with whatever software your business has decided to use to track their inventory and sales.

Familiarity with your systems is key to preventing cannabis from being hijacked down the supply chain or spoiling by taking up shelf space with products that should have cleared faster.

Financial ability to design, build and manage cannabis businesses

The application to obtain your license to grow or dispense cannabis includes many projects and plans for your facility and perhaps the packaging and labeling of the product. Designers are very important to the image and look they can convey for your new cannabis brand. So having them draw up plans for your property or product packaging won't be cheap. But if your application is successful, it gets even more expensive because projects now have to be built and used.

With or without access to loans and grants available to "qualified social equity applicants", all licensed cannabis companies must prove their financial capacity to carry out their projects and make them a reality. This cost is specific and unique to your particular brand, its design and the location of the properties.

Regardless of whether your cannabis business is highly cost-conscious or well-funded, you need to be able to demonstrate that you have the money to carry out your projects and application specifications, including financing for your operations.

Employee Handbook and Educational Policies Required by Illinois Cannabis Law

Many companies build their employment practices and manuals as they grow over time, but cannabis companies need to have them in place before opening their doors.

Training your cannabis employees is another step in setting your brand for the customer experience, but it also draws on your safety policies by teaching practices for observing the person's body language and actions to remember certain details, in case something goes wrong.

Additional employee education and training can guide policies to reduce and recognize theft and protect employees and customers in the event of a robbery.

Of course, budtenders should have knowledge of the flower and its extracts, terpenoid profiles and strains so that they can advise clients on what kind of experience they intend to gain from cannabis.

Employee training policies can help you make your customers happy, state regulators happy, and your business safe.

Community Commitment / Social Equity Plan to Achieve the Goals of the Illinois Cannabis Law

While not many points are specifically enumerated for community outreach, and in some cases the points are simply bonuses in the event of a tie, which means you should still do it. If you tied and didn't include it, but the other candidate did, bad luck!

What does your cannabis company do to give back? There are many things you can do to educate people, or help those harmed by the damage caused by the war on drugs, or another woman, minority, veteran or disabled group.
Provide funding for this engagement plan in your business operations budget, as it should be an ongoing expense that your business continues to make to enrich the community it serves.

Costs for employees of the cannabis dispensary

Dispensary managers must keep the business running smoothly and in a compliant manner. They deal with employees, customers, vendors, state regulators, business owners, perhaps even investors. They are in demand due to the scarcity of the industry, but consultants estimate that for a dispensary, annual staff costs can reach the range of a quarter of a million dollars.

Costs for your professional cannabis consultants

There are both upfront costs and ongoing costs. You need a lawyer, an accountant, an operations consultant and you need to be properly insured. Annual budgets for these range in the tens of thousands of dollars.

Costs to promote your cannabis business

Not just SEO, social media outreach, design and youTubes, you can sponsor community outreach events to build your brand. Our favorite is sponsoring expungement seminars and job fairs in partnership with local lawyer associations, politicians and cannabis companies. Remember to include these things in your plans and set yourself apart from the competition.

Summary of the costs of entering the legal cannabis market in Illinois

So now you understand why we said it would have averaged around $ 500,000 to open a cannabis dispensary in Illinois. We didn't actually get into all the costs of the growing craft equipment that can mount up due to the various HVAC and machinery, and the safety, construction requirements of a craft grow. That average will likely be around $ 2,000,000, but it depends on what features the grower wants to offer.

CHAPTER 11: HOW TO APPLY FOR A LICENSE IN MASSACHUSETTS

Applying for a Massachusetts cannabis license is the first step any cannabis entrepreneur residing in the Bay State should take. Lawmakers passed recreational cannabis legislation in July 2017.
The Cannabis Control Commission (CCC) is responsible for enacting marijuana regulations, processing corporate applications and licensing, and creating policies and procedures that "promote and encourage full participation in the regulated marijuana industry by people from communities that have previously been disproportionately harmed by the prohibition and application of marijuana and to have a positive impact on those communities.

Types of Massachusetts Cannabis Licenses

Marijuana Growing License. A marijuana grower can grow, process and package marijuana, to transfer and supply marijuana products to marijuana establishments, but not to consumers.

There are 11 levels of marijuana grower licenses depending on the canopy size the applicant would use:

Level 1: Up to 5,000 square feet
Level 2: 5.001 to 10,000 square feet
Level 3: 10,001 to 20,000 square feet
Level 4: 20,001 to 30,000 square feet
Level 5: 30,001 to 40,000 square feet
Level 6: 40,001 to 50,000 square feet
Level 7: From 50,001 to 60,000 square feet
Level 8: 60.001 to 70,000 square feet
Level 9: 70,001 to 80,000 square feet
Level 10: 80,001 to 90,000 square feet
Level 11: 90,001 to 100,000 square feet

Marijuana craft cooperative. A type of marijuana grower who can grow, obtain, produce, process, package and brand marijuana and marijuana products to supply marijuana to marijuana establishments, but not to consumers. To apply for this type of license, you need a team consisting of:

Massachusetts residents who have formed a limited liability company, limited liability partnership, or co-operative company;

A company can only have a Craft Marijuana Cooperative license;

Members of an artisanal marijuana cooperative cannot have a controlling interest in any other marijuana establishment;

An artisanal marijuana cooperative is not limited to a particular number of growing locations, but is limited to a total canopy of 100,000 square feet and three licensed business locations for manufacturers of marijuana products;

A member of the Craft Marijuana Cooperative must have filed a Schedule F (Farm Income Report) tax form within the past five years.

The Craft Marijuana Cooperative must operate according to the seven cooperative principles published by the International Cooperative Alliance in 1995.

Manufacturer of marijuana products. A marijuana product manufacturer is an entity authorized to obtain, manufacture, process and package marijuana and marijuana products, supply marijuana and marijuana products to marijuana establishments, and transfer marijuana and marijuana products to other marijuana establishments, but not to consumers.

Marijuana dealer. A marijuana dealer is an entity licensed to purchase and supply marijuana and marijuana products from marijuana establishments and to sell or otherwise transfer marijuana and marijuana products to marijuana establishments and to consumers.

Marijuana transporter. A marijuana transporter is an entity that can transport marijuana or marijuana products only when such transport is not already authorized under a Marijuana Establishment license if it is licensed as a marijuana transporter:

Third Party Transporter: An entity registered to do business in Massachusetts that does not hold another Marijuana Establishment license under 935 CMR 500,050 and is not registered as a registered marijuana dispensary under 105 CMR 725,000.

Existing licensed transporter: A marijuana establishment that wishes to contract with other marijuana establishments to transport their marijuana and marijuana products to other marijuana establishments.

Marijuana Research Center. A Marijuana Research Facility is an academic institution, a non-profit corporation, or a national corporation or entity licensed to do business in the Commonwealth of Massachusetts. A Marijuana Research Center may grow, purchase or otherwise acquire marijuana for the purpose of conducting research on marijuana and marijuana products. Any research involving humans must be authorized by an institutional review board. A marijuana research center cannot sell the marijuana it has grown.

Microbusiness marijuana. A micro-enterprise is a Tier 1 marijuana grower and / or co-located marijuana product manufacturer limited to purchasing 2,000 pounds of marijuana from other marijuana establishments in one year.

A Microbusiness licensee must not have an ownership stake in any other Marijuana Establishment and the majority of its executives or members must be resident in Massachusetts for no less than 12 months before the application can apply for a Microbusiness license.

CHAPTER 12: LICENSE FOR HEMP DISTRIBUTOR IN NEW YORK

New York lawmakers have created an adult use distributor license for those interested in starting a cannabis business to enter the industry. Following the unveiling of Bill S854, New York is on its way to becoming the sixteenth states to legalize recreational marijuana.

The Adult Use Distributor License is one of 10 types of cannabis licenses available in the Big Apple. And while we have to wait for the state to pass the bill and officially legalize cannabis for cannabis application in New York to open, we can give you information on the adult use distributor license to familiarize you and consider your options for starting your own. cannabis activity

What is an Adult Use Distributor License?

A distributor's license authorizes the acquisition, possession, distribution and sale of cannabis from the licensed premises of a licensed adult grower, processor, small adult-use cooperative or micro-enterprise licensed to sell adult-use cannabis, to duly authorized retail dispensaries.

"Distributor" means any person who wholesales any cannabis product, other than medical cannabis, for which a license is required under the provisions of this chapter.

"Wholesale" means soliciting or receiving an order to, hold or display for sale and hold with intent to sell, made by any authorized person, whether principal, owner, agent or employee of any adult use, medical cannabis or cannabis product or hemp cannabinoid product and hemp extract for resale purposes

Adult Use Distributor License Restrictions

No distributor is permitted to have a direct or indirect economic interest in any adult retail dispensary or any licensed adult grower or processor or any registered organization. This restriction does not prohibit a licensed registered organization from obtaining a license from the board of directors to distribute adult cannabis products grown and processed by the registered organization to licensed retail dispensaries for adult use owned and operated by such organizations.

A distributor will not be prevented from charging an appropriate, council-authorized fee for the distribution of cannabis, based on the volume of cannabis distributed.

CHAPTER 13: WHAT IS A DELIVERY LICENSE?

"Delivery" means the direct delivery of cannabis products by a retail licensee, micro enterprise licensee or delivery license holder to a cannabis user.

A delivery license will authorize delivery of cannabis and cannabis products by licensees independent of another adult-use cannabis license.

Limitations of the Cannabis Delivery License

No one may have a direct or indirect financial or controlling interest in more than one delivery license. These licenses are intended to promote applicants for social and economic equity as provided in this chapter.

Cannabis delivery license regulation

Once the bill is approved, the state cannabis advisory board will provide recommendations to the board for the application process, licensing criteria, and scope of licensed activities for this class of licensing. So far, no time frame has been set for the drafting of these regulations

Features of the delivery license
We will have to wait for the account to be approved before we learn more about the cannabis delivery license in New York. So far there isn't much information on what the license requirements and features are like.

Among the few rules already defined, the bill states that each delivery licensee can have a total of no more than twenty-five people, or the equivalent, providing paid, full-time delivery services per week with a license.

CHAPTER 14: GEORGIA MEDICAL CANNABIS PRODUCTION LICENSE

Georgia is accepting applications for licenses for the production of medical cannabis. After the state cleared the use of medical marijuana in 2015, the General Assembly finally passed a bill allowing the production and sale of marijuana in Georgia and applications are now open.

The Georgia Access to Medical Cannabis Commission has unanimously approved the process that will allow nearly 14,000 patients registered in Georgia to obtain oil for treatment in the state. Applications must be submitted on December 28th and with such a short time frame you should move quickly to submit your application on time. Production licenses are expected to be issued by March 2021.

Types of cannabis licenses in Georgia
Georgia Class 1 Medical Marijuana Producer License
The Class 1 production license authorizes a licensee to:

Grow cannabis only in indoor facilities for low-THC oil production, limited to 100,000 square feet of grow space

Make oil that is low in THC

The commission will issue two Class 1 production licenses.

Georgia Medical Marijuana Class 2 Producer License
The Class 2 Production License authorizes a licensee to:

Grow cannabis only in indoor facilities for low-THC oil production, limited to 50,000 square feet of grow space

Make oil that is low in THC

The Commission will issue four Class 2 production licenses.

Number of cannabis production licenses in Georgia

Georgia establishes a very limited number of licenses to be issued throughout the state. The state allows the issuance of six licenses for the cultivation of medical marijuana, which cannot contain more than 5% THC.

The commission will award licenses to two 100,000 square foot facilities and four 50,000 square foot facilities.

What cannabis products can a Class 1 and Class 2 medical marijuana licensee produce?

The laws of Georgia allow a Class 1 and Class 2 manufacturing license to produce low THC oil. Georgia law does not allow manufacturing licensees to make or produce cannatol, tinctures, topical, fast-onset sublingual, edible, inhalable products, etc. These products are banned for production and sale in Georgia.

Cost of medical cannabis production license in Georgia

A Class 1 production license requires a non-refundable subscription fee of $ 25,000, an initial license fee of $ 200,000, and a license renewal fee of $ 100,000.

A Class 2 production license requires a non-refundable application fee of $ 5,000, an initial license fee of $ 100,000, and a license renewal fee of $ 50,000.

Cannabis production license application process in Georgia

The application processes for both types of medical cannabis production licenses in Georgia are open to the general public.

Questionnaire for candidates

Those applying for a license to produce medical cannabis in Georgia must submit the following questionnaire which has been answered.

Schedule an Ownership Profile - Class 1 Production License

Schedule B Facility Information - Class 1 Production License

Schedule C Financial Information - Class 1 Production License

Schedule D Property Structure - Class 1 Production License

Schedule and Employment Plan - Class 1 Production License

Program F Local Government Support - Class 1 Production License

Production Plan Schedule G - Class 1 Production License

Plan Tracking Plan from Seed To Sale - Class 1 Production License

Schedule I Business Operations and Security Plan - Class 1 Production License

Applicants will need to ensure security at their facility, establish electronic video monitoring, and use magnetic cards that record employee and visitor access. Additionally, seed -to-sale monitoring is required to take into account the location of the product during production. Law enforcement officers must be able to inspect the facility upon request.
Is it possible to submit applications for both Class 1 and Class 2 production license?

Georgia law does not prohibit submitting a proposal for Class 1 and 2 production licenses. However, if a proposal for licensing in one class is selected, ownership interests in another class are prohibited.

"No person or entity that holds an ownership interest in a license issued under this section of the code may have an ownership interest in any other type of license under this part."

"Ownership interest in more than one license will cause all licenses to be revoked."

Does a production license include a dispensing license? A manufacturing license in Georgia does not include a dispensing license. The Commission has not yet established the requirements for the dispensing license or the rules for regulating medical cannabis dispensaries.

The dispensary license application process will begin in 2021 after the Class 2020 and Class 1 of 2 production license application cycle.

CHAPTER 15: GETTING A LICENSE IN MISSISSIPPI

It is proposed to amend the Mississippi constitution to allow qualified patients with debilitating medical conditions, as certified by licensed Mississippi physicians, to use medical marijuana. This amendment would allow medical marijuana to be provided only by the licensing processing center

The Mississippi Department of Health must implement the provisions of the amendment and issue rules and regulations for the program by July 1, 2021.

Deadline for issuing ID cards and health center licenses is August 15, 2021. Summer 2021 - Mississippi license application and submission window.

Types of commercial marijuana licenses to apply in Mississippi:

The only license available for a marijuana business in Mississippi is for " Medical Marijuana Treatment Center".

Medical Marijuana Treatment Centers are entities that are registered, licensed and regulated by the department and that process medical marijuana, related supplies and / or educational materials. A treatment center may have one or more activities involved in the processing of medical marijuana.

What is the number of commercial marijuana licenses allowed in Mississippi?

Mississippi has not established a limited number of statewide licenses for medical marijuana treatment centers, unlike many other states in the United States such as Illinois and Arizona.

Taxes in Mississippi for marijuana

The department can estimate up to the equivalent of the state sales tax rate for the final sale of medical marijuana, but the tax rate has not yet been established.

Municipalities can ban marijuana businesses in Mississippi

Local zoning regulations applicable to marijuana treatment centers cannot be more restrictive than other similarly sized and staffed legal commercial or industrial businesses.
First of all, you need the right cannabis business plan. As part of the program, you will clarify what

type of dispensary you want to open, how long you plan to operate in Mississippi, and what the main points of your business are.

When applying for a cannabis license in Mississippi or any state, the most important part of the process is following the regulations when it comes to the application form. It is always smart to consult an attorney about the regulations in a specific state.

Not all laws are the same in the United States, but most of them fall into the same category. Application requirements, required data and specific information about your business should always be at hand when applying for a dispensary license.

Pay attention to municipal regulations, some cities will have rules that may be more advantageous or very restrictive for your business. Make sure you are assisted in choosing your location

If you are unsure how to complete your application, you can contact the right attorney who will help you create the right plan for your application process when you want to open a cannabis dispensary in Mississippi.

CHAPTER 16: PENNSYLVANIA

Bearing in mind that the cannabis market in Pennsylvania will double sales over the next three to four years, hitting the $ 1 billion point, we need to consider all aspects of online and offline cannabis sales in this state.

How to measure adult cannabis use points in Pennsylvania?

According to the Marijuana Policy Draft Report, there are 102,000 medical patients in Pennsylvania. It represents 0.80% of the population of the state where medical marijuana was legalized on April 6, 2016, as part of the program approved by Governor Tom Wolf.

The Governor is now in favor of legalizing recreational cannabis as the forecasts presented in the financial plans say that sales will peak in the following years.

Today, in the state where the population reaches over 12 million people, many potential cannabis users are on the list for medical marijuana cards. At the same time, the recreational market is on the rise as the state wants to legalize recreational cannabis this year.

If the trend continues, Pennsylvania expects to have far more medical and recreational cannabis users.

What are the effective possession limits for cannabis in Pennsylvania?

Typical fines for marijuana possessions in Pennsylvania are between $ 25 and $ 500, which is still high if we know that many states have already fully legalized marijuana. Possession limits are 30 grams of cannabis.

Why do people in this state have to pay high fines for possessing marijuana?

It is part of Pennsylvania's social equity issues where we still have huge debates over the legalization of marijuana. One side of the coin is that legalization would bring far more problems than good, as many officials argue.

On the other hand, the decriminalization of cannabis in Pennsylvania would open up the market that could grow to over $ 2 billion, as many forecasts say at the moment.

If officials allow the decriminalization of cannabis, we will see why marijuana in Pennsylvania is one of the fastest growing industries in the years to come.

What is a "Use Lounge " in Pennsylvania?

"Use lounge." A space, determined by the department, where individuals can use the cannabis that individuals have brought into that space. The space can be public or private and can be owned by one person, including an individual, corporation, partnership, association, trust, government or other entity, or any combination of these. The space can be shared with, attached to, or adjacent to a dispensary, in which case the dispensary may require that users of the use room only use cannabis sold by the dispensary while on the premises of the use room.

How to open a dispensary in Pennsylvania

To open a dispensary in Pennsylvania, you'll need to abide by the state's regulatory rules. It means that an applicant must be at least 21 years old and must pay a non-refundable application fee of $ 5,000.

Accordingly, the application will be submitted to the Pennsylvania Department of Health, where applicants will submit their requests. Permits will be issued for a limited number of dispensaries and the lucky candidates will have to fight for a total of 50 dispensaries. Each dispensary must have no more than 3 locations in the state of Pennsylvania. Additional requirements for opening a dispensary in Pennsylvania are:

Ability to maintain security measures within the dispensary

Provision of a diversity plan

Have a business organization plan

Paying the $ 30,000 authorization fee

Proof of $ 150,000 in total capital

Meeting all of these requirements will give you the chance to win one of Pennsylvania's popular dispensary licenses. Only 50 will be released this year, while the number of applicants vastly exceeds this number.

How to get a microgrowers license in Pennsylvania?

Getting a microgrowers license in Pennsylvania is relatively easy if you follow the official recommendations. The rules propose that up to 150 plants can be grown under the cultivation license.

At the same time, licenses are limited to three per person. A large grow unit can grow cannabis up to 150,000 square feet, which applies to outdoor growing.

Smaller units are limited to 60,000 square feet per business unit where marijuana is grown indoors.
When it comes to adult cannabis use in Pennsylvania, growers will grow up to 10 cannabis plants with an entry fee of $ 50 annually.

All of these requirements are still under review by the local government. Some changes will no doubt apply in the future as the cannabis market in Pennsylvania continues to grow with a speed we haven't seen recently in any other state.

CHAPTER 17: HOW TO GET A LICENSE IN SOUTH DAKOTA

South Dakota went from zero to one hundred with its cannabis laws! - Going from having no legalization of any kind to passing two new laws that allow both medical and recreational marijuana in the state, you can finally get a marijuana license to operate in South Dakota.

South Dakota voted to pass Amendment A which legalized recreational marijuana with a 54-46% vote. Measure 26 to legalize medical marijuana has also been passed, but by a wider margin of 70 to 30 percent.

The cannabis market is opening up in the state, it is your opportunity to start preparing your license application to open your cannabis business. Don't forget, the cannabis industry is very complicated and has many complicated rules. We have all the details you need to be aware of if you are interested in obtaining a cannabis license in South Dakota

The regulations are still being drafted, so we can expect many changes in the following years. The Department of Revenue is the regulatory authority for the recreational cannabis program in South Dakota, responsible for licensing applications, while the MMJ program would be regulated by the South Dakota Department of Health.

The legalization of South Dakota will become law on July 1, 2021. The Department of Revenue will be tasked with developing licensing regulations by April 1, 2022.

Types of marijuana licenses to apply for in South Dakota

For the recreational marijuana program, the licenses available in South Dakota under Amendment A are:

License to grow, process, produce, transport and sell marijuana to marijuana wholesalers;
Licenses that allow independent marijuana testing facilities to analyze and certify the safety and potency of marijuana;
License to package, process and prepare marijuana for transportation and sale to retail outlets;
License that allows retail stores to sell and supply marijuana to consumers.
Other types of licenses may be established by the department

The license available for the medical marijuana program:
Licensing for medical marijuana dispensaries would be regulated by the South Dakota Department of Health. The local government can set a limit on the number of medical cannabis establishments in your locality

What is the number of licenses allowed for the cannabis industry in South Dakota?
South Dakota hasn't established a limited number of state-level licenses, unlike many other states in the United States such as Illinois and Arizona.
While it has no state-wide limit on the number of licenses approved for either medical marijuana companies or adult-use businesses, cities can govern their own numbers.

How much does a marijuana license cost in South Dakota?

Obviously, the cost of a cannabis license will depend on the type of license you wish to obtain for your operation. We still don't have a number for the cost of licenses as regulations are still being written.

Amendment A states that by April 2022 the Department is expected to enact the necessary regulations for licensing, renewal, suspension and revocation of licenses, including applications, qualifications and fees, so stay tuned!

What are the requirements to apply for a marijuana license in South Dakota?

Qualifications for licensees;

Security requirements, including lighting and alarm requirements, to prevent irregularities;

Testing, packaging and labeling requirements, including maximum levels of tetrahydrocannabinol, to ensure consumer safety and accurate information;

Restrictions on the production and sale of edible products to ensure the safety of consumers and children;
Health and safety requirements to ensure safe preparation and ban unsafe pesticides;
Inspection, traceability and recording requirements to ensure regulatory compliance and prevent deviation;
Restrictions on advertising and marketing;

Requirements to ensure that all applicable legal requirements relating to the environment, agriculture and food and product safety are met;

Requirements to prevent the sale and diversion of marijuana to persons under the age of 21

Taxes in South Dakota for marijuana

The amendment imposes a 15% tax on marijuana sales. The tax revenue will be used for the Department's expenses, with the remaining revenue split equally between public school support and the state general fund.

How to start preparing your marijuana application

First of all, you need the right cannabis business plan. As part of the program, you will clarify what type of dispensary you want to open, how long you plan to operate in South Dakota, and what the main points of your business are.

If you are starting your cannabis business and want more focus, we recommend our pitch deck course, it would be a great opportunity for you to start imagining your own cannabis dispensary.

When applying for a cannabis license in South Dakota or any state, the most important part of the process is following the regulations when it comes to the application form. It is always smart to consult a lawyer regarding the regulations in a specific state.

Not all laws are the same in the United States, but most of them fall into the same category. Application requirements, required data and specific information about your business should always be at hand when applying for a dispensary license.

South Dakota key point CONSTITUTIONAL AMENDMENT A AND MEASURE 26

The legalization of South Dakota will become law on July 1, 2021. The Department of Revenue will be tasked with developing licensing regulations by April 1, 2022.

Growing at home in South Dakota

MIN 4 plants
Amendment A: 3 plants per adult, 6 per family IF you live in an area without a licensed retail store
Social equity in South Dakota cannabis laws?
Bare minimum criteria towards restorative justice:

Expungement? NO

Social equity provisions? NO
Portion of taxes allocated to the community? NO

South Dakota cannabis possession rules
MAX 3 oz
Amendment A: MAX 1 oz

Licenses available:
Amendment A:
License to grow, process, produce, transport and sell marijuana to marijuana wholesalers;
Licenses that allow independent marijuana testing facilities to analyze and certify the safety and potency of marijuana;
License to package, process and prepare marijuana for transportation and sale to retail outlets;
License that allows retail stores to sell and supply marijuana to consumers.
Other types of licenses may be established by the department

Rule 26:
Licensing for medical marijuana dispensaries would be regulated by the South Dakota Department of Health. The local government can set a limit on the number of medical cannabis establishments in your locality

Amendment A states that by April 2022 the Department is expected to issue the necessary regulations for licensing, renewal, suspension and revocation of licenses, including applications, qualifications and fees.

The time period could not exceed 90 days, at which point the Department must have issued an answer on the application, either accepting or rejecting it.

No limited number of state-level licenses: cities can regulate the number.

CHAPTER 18: HOW TO GET A LICENSE IN FRESNO IN CALIFORNIA

Well, we can think of California as the OG of cannabis in America and the dawn of the legal cannabis industry, but still more than half of the counties in the state have outlawed the plant. In early 2019, the Marijuana Business newspaper reported that only 161 of the 482 municipalities and only 24 of the 58 counties allow commercial cannabis in California, which means that all Republican areas of the state have yet to legalize it, while it may not be the case, the more rural and conservative parts of the state won't allow it - which brings us to Fresno!

Before you think this is Trump's country - it's not - Hillary Clinton won Fresno County in 2016. Proposal 64 was only approved by 1% and, 4 years later, we are preparing to let go of applications. However, California isn't exactly a red state, but the sheer number of bans across the state shows the bias we're fighting against when it comes to the plant.

So now we will talk about how to open a cannabis dispensary in Fresno California.

In California, they put the cornerstone of cannabis at the center - it's all local. The local municipality or county has the power to obtain the license, so after obtaining the license, you must re-register with the state. Because what's better than a big regulatory column to overcome when trying to sell a plant that has never killed anyone from overdose - it's true. 2 normative sections.

What do we do then, let's go to the municipal ordinance and related regulations from their municipal code? And when we dig deeper - we realize what is likely to happen throughout the rest of California when it gets legalized - there will be A LOT of regulations.

How many regulations - well, you have to tackle the NIMBY effect front and center. Let's go to the Fresno Code of Ordinances, Section 15-5001 - Item 50 - Common Procedures. it covers the common procedures for applying for all permits and approvals - yes, it could be a public hearing. And you have to follow it to get your conditional cannabis use permit application on file with Fresno.

The application for conditional use of cannabis must be accompanied by a written narrative, operational statement, floor plans, prospectuses and other evidence to support the applicable findings by the municipality. You need a public hearing to get permission - and to indemnify the city against the feds or something on the way - which is silly, they want your tax money, but they also want you to protect them if the feds decide to shut you down. A good community would reverse the situation and promise to use some of the tax proceeds to pressure the feds to change their crazy unconstitutional law. But I'm digressing. You have to do it 100% to get your license, so do it, so try to see if you can organize lobbying days with your congressman and senator to get federal law changed.

Let's see what the rest of the cannabis retail ordinance draft in Fresno, CA covers. You will see that there are four main parts of the license and a standard legislative tapestry. The ordinance directs you to other sections of their code - which has an interesting naming convention - you need to go to Section 9 - Article 33 of the Code. Some of the sections are the same for any cannabis business, but some are relevant to the type of business license you want. For example, dispensaries need definitions, but also the commercial permit for cannabis which requires:

(1) a valid commercial trade permit for cannabis from the city;

(2) a valid state license;

(3) a valid cannabis conditional use permit;

(4) it currently complies with all applicable state and local laws;

(5) a tax certificate for the commercial cannabis license.

So, you need to secure signage, building, lighting, and more for your conditional cannabis use permit, including the following:

A written narrative
Operational statement
Site plans
Floor plans

Other evidence supporting other findings required by section 15-5306 of their code.
The proposed use is permitted within the applicable zoning district and complies with all other applicable provisions of this Code and all other chapters of the Municipal Code;

The proposed use is consistent with the General Plan and any other applicable plans and design guidelines that the City has adopted;

The proposed use will not be materially detrimental to the public health, safety or general welfare of the community, nor will it be harmful to surrounding properties or improvements;

The design, location, size and operational characteristics of the proposed activity are compatible with existing and reasonably foreseeable future land uses in the vicinity;

The site is physically suitable for the proposed type, density and intensity of use, including access, emergency access, public utilities and required services;

The proposed use is consistent with the Fresno County Airport Land Use Compatibility Plan (which may be amended) adopted by the Fresno County Airport Land Use Commission in accordance with sections of the California Utilities Code 21670-21679.5.

You see - this is exactly why the cost of licensing is tens of thousands of dollars and many in the Californian market may choose to stay in the legacy market - we must fight the ongoing stigma against the plant to make it just as easy to get. a liquor license as for obtaining a commercial license for cannabis. But let's take it one day at a time and move on to the additional regulations your cannabis dispensary in Fresno California will need, returning to Article 33 of the code:

It is necessary to respect:
All article 33 - we will list those for dispensaries:

Compliance with lase 9-3303

Definitions 9-3304

Company permits required - 9-3305

Maximum limits - 9-3306

Location and design for retail cannabis 9-3307

Operational Requirements for All Cannabis Businesses 9-3309

And the most important - operational requirements for cannabis retail - 9-3310

But don't forget social fairness: it's in the initial application procedures in 9-3316.

Of course, there are more, such as bans, renewal, change of position, initial application process, registration and record keeping,

Hence, the ordinance itself goes beyond social equity and neighborhood accountability plans as well. Now these plans are buried in the sections I recited earlier - they go into much more detail about your neighborhood plans, your security plans as required by the operational plan, and social equity as in the initial application process.

The social fairness aspect of licensing requires the minimum of some types of historically voting people, a peace deal at work, social responsibility plans, and even a social equity applicant who will receive at least 1 in 7 questions.

So, there you have it - I could have spent another half hour spitting out the straight text of this very complex licensing scheme that Fresno - and probably the next California city has for their cannabis retail licenses. The remaining areas of the state are all more conservative, which means more regulation.

CHAPTER 19: HOW TO OBTAIN A COMMERCIAL LICENSE OF CANNABIS IN MONTANA

Get ready to start preparing your cannabis business license application in Montana! Montana is one of five states, alongside Arizona, Mississippi, New Jersey, and South Dakota, to have passed bills legalizing cannabis in the 2020 elections.

Montana passed Initiative I-190 with a victory margin of 57 to 43 percent. People in Montana will be able to apply for a commercial cannabis license and start operating in the state very soon.

Montana's Cannabis I-190 Initiative is expected to generate approximately $ 48 million annually in tax revenue and licensing fees by 2025.

The Montana Cannabis Initiatives take effect on January 1, 2021. No later than October 1, 2021, the department must enact rules and regulations for license applications. The rules may not be overly burdensome.

It is estimated that the department will begin accepting applications for suppliers and dispensaries on January 1, 2022. For the first 12 months after the department begins receiving applications, it will only issue licenses to suppliers,

suppliers of marijuana products and dispensaries already licensed.

Types of commercial cannabis licenses in Montana

Dispensaries: Registered premises from which an authorized supplier for adult use or a supplier of marijuana products for adult use is authorized to dispense marijuana or marijuana products to consumers

Test laboratories: to perform the tests required by the Department

Licensing Providers: Person authorized by the department to grow and process marijuana for consumers

Marijuana Product Suppliers: Person authorized by the department to manufacture and supply marijuana products for consumers

The latter two types of licenses will be issued under the tiered coverage system:

 A micro level canopy license allows for a canopy of up to 250 square feet in a registered location.

A level 1 canopy license allows for a canopy of up to 1,000 square feet in a registered location. A minimum of 500 square feet must be equipped for cultivation.

A level 2 canopy license allows for a canopy of up to 2,500 square feet in up to two registered locations. A minimum of 1,100 square feet must be equipped for cultivation.

A level 3 canopy license allows for a canopy of up to 5,000 square feet in up to three registered locations. A minimum of 2,600 square feet must be equipped for cultivation.

A level 4 canopy license allows for a canopy of up to 7,500 square feet in up to four registered locations. A minimum of 5,100 square feet must be equipped for cultivation.

A level 5 canopy license allows coverage of up to 10,000 square feet in up to five registered locations. A minimum of 7,750 square feet must be equipped for cultivation.

A level 6 canopy license allows coverage of up to 13,000 square feet in up to five registered locations. A minimum of 10,250 square feet must be equipped for cultivation.

A level 7 canopy license allows coverage of up to 15,000 square feet in up to five registered locations. A minimum of 13,250 square feet must be equipped for cultivation.

A level 8 canopy license allows coverage of up to 17,500 square feet in up to five registered locations. A minimum of 15,250 square feet must be equipped for cultivation.

A level 9 canopy license allows for a canopy of up to 20,000 square feet in up to six registered locations. A minimum of 17,775 square feet must be equipped for cultivation.

A level 10 canopy license allows for a canopy of up to 30,000 square feet in up to seven registered locations. A minimum of 24,000 square feet must be equipped for cultivation.

Requirements for applying for a commercial cannabis license in Montana

The name, date of birth and address of the person on a form prescribed by the department;

proof that the person is a resident of Montana;

digital fingerprint

the address of the location where marijuana, marijuana concentrates or marijuana products will be grown or manufactured;

A fee that does not exceed the required background check costs and associated administrative costs for license processing.

If the application is for more than one person, the names of all owners must be presented along with each owner's fingerprints and date of birth.

The department cannot license a person if the person or owner:

Has a conviction for a crime involving fraud, deception or embezzlement or for distributing drugs to a minor within the past 5 years and,

Has resided in Montana for less than 1 year;

He is under 18.

Marijuana must be grown and produced in Montana until federal law allows interstate distribution of marijuana

Social Equity Program in Montana

The provisions on social equity to be implemented in Montana are not mentioned in the full text of initiative no. I 190. However, the initiative requires that a portion of the taxes be allocated to affected communities and allows for petitioning for the lifting of previous cannabis-related convictions.

Part of the taxes will go to "Substance Abuse Treatment and Prevention Funding, funding veterans' programs to compensate for previous uses of unregulated marijuana in ways that have harmed veterans, funding for locations where marijuana is sold to offset the costs associated with marijuana regulation, and funding for the general fund to account for any costs to the state arising from the use and regulation of marijuana. "

Commercial cannabis license in Montana for out-of-state investors?

It requires marijuana supplier licenses to be issued only to residents of the state.

An individual is not considered a resident if the individual:

Applies for residency in another state or country for any purpose; or

He is an absentee owner who pays property tax on the Montana property.

Taxes in Montana for cannabis

Under the initiative, a 20% tax on non-medicinal marijuana will be established. 10.5% of the tax revenue will go to the state general fund. The rest is devoted to conservation programs, substance abuse treatment, veteran services, healthcare costs, and locations where marijuana is sold.

The rest would be distributed among community college districts, fire and police departments, and other grants or programs in support of public health.

Municipalities can ban commercial cannabis licenses in Montana

You may not be able to get licensed anywhere in Montana. This Montana cannabis initiative allows individual counties to ban dispensaries through a public vote.

How can I start preparing my cannabis corporate license application?

First of all, you need the right cannabis business plan. As part of the program, you will clarify what type of dispensary you want to open, how long you plan to operate in Montana, and what the main points of your business are.

If you are starting your cannabis business and want more focus, we recommend our pitch deck course, it would be a great opportunity for you to start imagining your own cannabis dispensary.

When applying for a cannabis license in Montana or any state, the most important part of the process is following the regulations when it comes to the application form. It is always smart to consult an attorney about the regulations in a specific state.

Not all laws are the same in the United States, but most of them fall into the same category. Application requirements, required data and specific information about your business should always be at hand when applying for a dispensary license.

Pay attention to municipal regulations, some cities will have rules that may be more advantageous or very restrictive for your business. Make sure you are assisted in choosing your location

Key points on Montana INITIATIVE I-190

Montana passed Initiative I-190 with a victory margin of 57 to 43 percent. The Montana initiatives will take effect on January 1, 2021.

Can it be grown in Montana?
YES, up to 4 plants per adult, max 8 plants per family

Social equity in Montana?
Bare minimum criteria towards restorative justice:
Expungement? YUP
Social equity provisions? NO
Part of the taxes allocated to affected communities? YUP
A portion of the fees will go to "substance abuse treatment and education, veteran programs"

Rules of possession
Up to 1 oz of flowers or 8 grams of concentrate

Cannabis Business License Windows in Montana

Montana will begin accepting applications for suppliers and dispensaries on January 1, 2022.

Cannabis corporate licenses available in Montana:
dispensaries
Test laboratories
Licensing suppliers and suppliers of marijuana products

CHAPTER 20: HOW TO BECOME A BUDTENDER

As an industry expands, the demand for skilled and enthusiastic workers increases. As the cannabis industry continues to develop, the need for cannabis enthusiasts and experts is emerging to perform various duties, including doctors and lab technicians, salespeople and writers. But how does one become a Budtender?
The budtender is perhaps one of the most accessible jobs related to cannabis. It has attracted the attention of many cannabis fanatics, both young and old. But what are the requirements for getting a job behind the counter at your local dispensary?

WHO IS THE BUDTENDER?

The budtenders are expert cannabis professionals, who work behind the counter of marijuana dispensaries in legal and regulated markets.
The best way to fully understand the role of the budtender is to imagine him as a kind of sommelier in a luxury restaurant or wine shop. Just like a sommelier, budtenders have extensive knowledge of all the products on sale in their shop. Their role

is to help customers choose the product that best suits their needs. The ideal budtender has a full knowledge of cannabis and the different strains. He is constantly updated on new trends in the cannabis industry.
In short, budtending seems like a really tempting job. But what are the skills needed to be able to work in a dispensary?

First of all, in our opinion the first step to becoming a budtender is having a great passion for cannabis. You can't expect to be tasked with recommending the right product to hundreds of users if you don't have a burning desire yourself to understand weed in its entirety. You will need to build trust with your customers. This will not be possible if you are unable to express the passion you have for the products you sell.

An equally essential aspect of becoming a budtender is full knowledge of the product. You wouldn't be able to apply to sell craft beer if you can't tell the difference between an IPA and a Porter. Likewise, you can't be a budtender without having a solid knowledge of cannabis. Even if you are not familiar with every variety grown on the planet in detail, you should at least have a fair knowledge of the most emblematic varieties, and of the latest products such as concentrates, vaporizers, etc.

The third key to becoming a budtender is being willing to constantly learn. We said earlier that it is quite unlikely that anyone will know all the ins and outs of every strain, old and new, and / or cannabis product launched on the market. After all, the cannabis sector is still very young. New products, new laws, new standards emerge every day. However, what characterizes an excellent budtender is their willingness to learn the latest in the industry, and keep themselves constantly updated on new products, innovations, and / or laws.

Last but not least, you can never become a budtender without excellent customer service skills. You will need to have the patience and the right ways to deal with customers of all kinds, including those who have just discovered cannabis and those who believe they already know it perfectly.

QUALIFICATIONS / CERTIFICATIONS

Some employers may be looking for budtenders with some type of certification and / or qualification. This is a gray area, and there are many variables between employers and states.

Your best bet is to talk to someone who has a dispensary in your area, and ask them about the documents or forms needed to work behind the counter, and where to find them.

WHERE TO LOOK FOR WORK

So, we talked about the skills we think are necessary to become a budtender. But where can you really go to look for work?

The development of the cannabis industry has given rise to various job posting sites dedicated to the industry. You can also search for cannabis related keywords in regular job postings. However, you may have a better chance at ad sites specifically dedicated to weed.

Probably the best way to find a job as a budtender or other cannabis-related job is to go directly to a dispensary. This will show your confidence and conviction. In addition, it will give you the opportunity to meet people who actively work in the field. Also, the cannabis sector is still new and small. Hence, many people will know someone who can point you in the right direction to find work.

Search beyond your borders

The cannabis industry in the United States is in full swing. But the US is not the only place where you can get experience becoming a budtender. Even in some places like the Netherlands and Spain cannabis is tolerated, up to certain levels. So, these too are ideal places to look for work and gain experience.

For example, coffeeshops in Amsterdam attract hundreds of thousands of international visitors every year. They are popular for offering some of the best cannabis in the world. In Amsterdam there are many coffeeshops where budtenders speak English. Knowledge of the Dutch language is not always required.

In recent years there has been a great growth of smoking clubs in Spain. Here cannabis users can legally enjoy premium weed without any risk of legal repercussions. According to many people, Spain is a beautiful place to live. Getting a job at one of these clubs really feels heavenly. However, keep in mind that knowledge of the Spanish language will probably be a necessary requirement.

There are many other nations now on the path to legalizing recreational marijuana. For example,

Uruguay intends to start selling cannabis legally through pharmacies in mid-2017. This could be another good opportunity for budding budtenders.

Having worked abroad is always a positive element to include in your CV. The cannabis industry is no exception. If you are not worried about trying your luck outside your homeland, try moving abroad. It could be the start of your long and successful career in the hemp industry

CHAPTER 21: WORKING WITH CANNABIS

There has never been a better time to translate your passion for cannabis into a job you love, instead of one that only pays the bills. The legal cannabis industry is growing at a rapid pace, and this pace is only expected to accelerate as judicious legalization reform continues to spread. By 2027, legal marijuana sales are expected to reach $ 57 billion. By then, North American consumers are expected to make up the largest clientele, with the rest of the world rapidly closing the gap.

Companies of all sizes are working hard to gain a share of the market, but they can't do it without skilled workers. The total number of cannabis-related jobs grew by 690% between January 1, 2017 and August 1, 2018, and wages increased by 16.1%. By 2021, experts predict that more than 400,000 people will be employed in the framework of the legal cannabis industry.

Experience and skills can help you land a job in the cannabis industry, but they are no longer a prerequisite. The demand for motivated workers is so high that cannabis companies have no choice but to provide new candidates with on-the-job training if they hope to fill all of their vacant positions. What's more, they also need people who don't work directly with marijuana plants. Commercial skills, such as accounting, customer service, marketing, and scheduling rank high on the list of jobs sought.

HOW TO ENTER THE CANNABIS INDUSTRY

1. THE TRADITIONAL JOB SEARCH STILL WORKS

Cannabis jobs have nothing to do with some sort of big secret club designed to keep you out of it. Traditional job search methods still work. If you live in an area where medicinal or recreational cannabis is legal, peruse classifieds, online job vacancies, and keep your eyes peeled for "help wanted" signs. You may even find work by walking into a store that interests you and submitting an application.

Announcement boards also offer many opportunities. There are quite a few sites that are specific to cannabis jobs, but employers who want to hire a lot of people might post ads on generalist recruiting sites as well. Recruiters, as well as recruiting agencies, are also on the hunt for new talent. If you are not sure exactly which job you would like, a temporary employment could help you narrow down the possible jobs that would suit you the most.

2. GROW YOUR KNOWLEDGE ABOUT CANNABIS

While looking for your dream job, take the time to learn as much as you can about cannabis, local legislation, and the companies you would most like to work with. Even if you are not an expert, and even if you are not a consumer, this will show your prospective employer that you are motivated and are really investing in this career choice.

Furthermore, this is one of the most regulated industries in the world. If you are applying for any job that requires you to make decisions that could put the company at risk, the interviewer is more likely to hire you if they feel that you know what is acceptable, and what is not, in the eyes of the law. This applies to positions at all levels, from the dispensary clerk to the executive administrator.

3. GROW RELATIONSHIPS AND CREATE CONNECTIONS

As with any industry, getting a job at a cannabis company may depend on who you know rather than what you know. Be friendly but also professional, whether you are visiting a local dispensary, a cannabis festival or a regional fair. Don't nag, but let it be clear that you are very interested in getting into the field. Not only will you learn where job postings are most likely to appear first, whether online or in a physical location, but a new contact may call you the first time they have an opportunity, or hear about it. Moreover, in any profession it never hurts to know who the insiders are.

If you don't have the opportunity to connect in person, follow the companies you would most like to work with on social media. On occasion, they publish lists of vacancies and other functions online.

4. BE FLEXIBLE!

The cannabis industry is an emerging sector of our economy, and the companies involved are changing the way they do business even faster than they are growing. They need people who are able to adapt quickly to ever-changing job roles, and who can improvise. This can give candidates who have worked for startup companies in the past an advantage over those with experience in large companies. In any case, even large corporations regularly put their employees in turmoil these days. During your job interview, be prepared to provide examples of how you found yourself having to be flexible in previous jobs.

5. MEET ALL LEGAL AND TRAINING REQUIREMENTS

If you are looking to get hired in an area where you need to be registered or certified to be able to work legally, do so before applying for a job. For example, anyone who wants to work with marijuana in Nevada must have a state-issued professional card. Candidates go through a thorough check of their path during the approval process. The card also specifies what kind of work the holder can carry out. For example, pruners have to work in the field of industry inherent to cultivation, while "cane-salesmen" can only work in the dispensary.

THE JOBS IN THE CANNABIS SECTOR, AND HOW MUCH THEY ARE PAID

1. PRUNERS: $ 12– $ 18 PER HOUR

This is probably the lowest paid job you can find in the cannabis industry, but it's also the easiest to get. However, it is not easy to do. Pruning, in case you've never done it, is hard work. Ask any grower, and 9 times out of 10 he'll tell you it's the thing he least likes to do. This job requires no experience. It can be seasonal in areas with large outdoor crops, and in addition to pruning you could also be used for harvesting and packaging.

Due to the nature of this work, pruners work on site. The best places to find a pruner job are in "legal states", such as California, Colorado and Washington State, but Canada, Holland, Germany, and Switzerland also hire pruners.

2. DELIVERY TRUCK DRIVERS: $ 14– $ 16 PER HOUR + TIPS IF ALLOWED

In areas where it is legal, customers can order dried, edible and concentrated flowers online and have them delivered to their home like a pizza. The delivery guy is the one who makes it possible. This job requires a good driving record and a reliable vehicle in case one is not provided. In urban areas, the person carrying out the deliveries might move around by bicycle like couriers. This is a basic position. Experience with cannabis might be an advantage, but not an essential requirement. The ability to use a GPS, follow directions and be reliable is much more important.

By definition, a delivery man has to work in close proximity to the product and customers, but this worker will be around for most of the day. California and Washington DC are great places to look for bellhop jobs; both of these areas have thriving home delivery services.

3. CANNABIS-ORDERS: $ 32,000– $ 42,000 PER YEAR

The "cannabis-salesmen" or " budtenders " are more than just salesmen and cashiers: they listen to the customer's needs and help him choose the most suitable herb. If necessary, they can also "educate" customers on why one type of cannabis is "better" than another in certain cases. Salesmen often help their customers find new ways to use cannabis, and recommend other products. They are some of the most knowledgeable workers in the cannabis industry, and the most experienced of them are often able to choose where they will go to work themselves.

This is another job that takes place on site. Salesmen work in dispensaries, and are the face of this industry. It is a popular career choice, especially in places like California, Oregon,

Colorado, Michigan, and other states where cannabis is frequently used for medicinal purposes. As legalization expands, new opportunities will open up for cannabis-committed jobs.

4. WEBSITE MANAGER AND CONTENT AUTHORS: $ 30,000– $ 70,000 PER YEAR

Cannabis companies of all kinds need a healthy online presence to thrive. It is reassuring for the public to know that this is legal business, and it helps build the brand. Website, social media and email correspondence managers generate an image of transparency, while content writers and editors educate customers about the industry itself and cannabis in general. Skills in digital marketing, graphic design, website design and text editing are required.

This type of employment allows you to work remotely while living anywhere in the world, even an area where cannabis is totally illegal. Established brands have the biggest budgets for their website, but a startup will have less competition for jobs.

5. EDIBLE PRODUCTS OR CANNA-CHEF PREPARER: $ 40,000– $ 90,000 PER YEAR

Edible preparations are incredibly popular, whether it's ganja candy, baked goods, or cannabis-infused drinks. And someone has to prepare them! The requirements for this job are experience in food safety, and in some cases a cooking school. Independent chefs and artisans who prepare edibles who work for established brands are the ones who earn the most, while those who work for smaller and emerging companies earn the least.

As long as you can get hold of cannabis isolates or extracts, you can make edibles and medicines wherever it is legal to do so. Your kitchen doesn't have to be near the grow site, or a dispensary. And indeed, under health regulations, it probably shouldn't be. Edibles are very popular in states where medical marijuana has been legal for some time, such as California and Colorado, so these are the best places to start your job search. In other places it is slowly catching up.

6. DIRECTOR OF COMPLIANCE: $ 45,000– $ 149,000

If you're not cool enough to get a job with a real cannabis company, look for a job in the compliance directorate of the regulatory committee. It will be your responsibility to ensure that every business in your district complies with all regulations that are in effect at any given time. You will meet a lot of insiders, and you will learn a lot about cannabis and the legal system.

The requirements include a certain level of legal knowledge and, in many cases, a degree. Job opportunities will be found in states or countries that have a strong legal cannabis industry with a high level of government control.

7. EXTRACTION DIRECTOR: $ 47,000– $ 191,000

Your job will be to direct the lower-level mining engineers, maintain quality and compliance, and develop better ways of producing dab, Budder, waxes and the like. Working for a small company will give you more control over your work, with a lower average salary, while jobs in larger companies can mean more oversight and reporting tasks, in exchange for higher compensation.

Extracts have been around for centuries in the form of hash, but Colorado has turned mining into an art form. Today there is a high demand for skilled craftsmen, as well as for their products, all over the world. For these types of job options, look for areas where cannabis is legal.

8. DISPENSARY MANAGER: $ 60,000– $ 150,000

A dispensary manager is responsible for maintaining stock levels, making sure the flowers are fresh, training employees and managing their shifts, and all other daily dispensary activities. He must also make sure that the dispensary operates within the legal deadlines.

Dispensary manager is a field job that can usually be found in legal states where dispensaries are licensed to operate.

9. CANNABIS GROWER: FROM $ 50,000 TO OVER A MILLION $ A YEAR

Growing cannabis is no longer delegated to an underground network of outlaws. It is now a legitimate career choice, which can be very profitable. If you grow on behalf of a company you can earn a good salary, but nowhere near what you would earn if you were an independent grower. The total amount you can earn in a year also depends on the laws in force in the place where you are operating. In some places there is a limit on the amount a single person can grow and sell, or even the people to whom it can be sold. Prices are also controlled in certain places.

The growers also work on site. The best places to work in cultivation are California, Colorado, Oregon, Michigan, Canada, Spain, and Uruguay. In-depth cannabis knowledge, high growing experience, and the ability to solve current problems are prerequisites.

10. DISPENSARY OWNER: UP TO $ 1,000,000 PER YEAR AND MORE

If you have the money to open a dispensary, there is virtually no limit to how much you can earn in return for dealing with all the licensing and legal hassle it entails. At this level, work has less to do with cannabis, and more to do with all the management tasks associated with running any medium or large business, but it also comes with one of the highest salary potentials in the industry. Of course, this also carries the greatest risks.

The owner of a small dispensary often makes sure to visit his establishment regularly, but he knows that it is not necessary to spend every hour of working time on the site, especially if he has a competent and loyal staff. The dispensary itself must be located in a state or country where it is legal to operate.

SUMMING UP

Over the past decade, the cannabis industry has exploded, and new job opportunities seem endless. This is the time to introduce yourself and participate in the early development of rapidly evolving companies, to become a respected expert in this field, even if you know very little about it at the moment. Develop your skills, be creative with your applications, and you may be rewarded with a lucrative new job in a field you love!

CHAPTER 22: HOW TO OPEN A CONSUMER ROOM IN DETROIT

Marijuana halls are now legal in Detroit. The city just passed the Detroit Legacy Marijuana Ordinance to legalize and regulate adult-use marijuana and licensing procedures. If you're interested in opening a marijuana parlor in Detroit, we have the information you need.

One of the coolest aspects of this new regulation is that the city will allow 35 consumer lounge licenses. Known in the new Detroit ordinance as Designated Consumption Establishments, consumer lounges are commercial spaces where adults are legally allowed to consume marijuana products, usually paying a fee to enter the establishment. But consumption rooms aren't necessarily licensed to sell cannabis and cannabis products, like dispensaries in Michigan.

"Designated Consumption Establishment" means a commercial space authorized by the agency and authorized to allow adults 21 years of age and older to consume marijuana products at the location indicated on the state license.

Cannabis consumption halls or designated establishments hail from Detroit understanding the conflict generated by the lack of places to consume cannabis other than private property and how it often causes an increase in arrests for possession, representatives deemed necessary to regulate places licensed to allow for public social gatherings where marijuana consumption was permitted.

This license is available to any applicant; no other licenses are required. But it is also available to marijuana retailers, micro-businesses, or anyone who wishes to operate under this model.

CHAPTER 23: NEW JERSEY CANNABIS MICRO ENTERPRISE LICENSE

The New Jersey cannabis microbusiness license is an intriguing option for small business owners in the state. New Jersey cannabis licensing regulations aim to benefit its residents with an exclusive opportunity to enter the market without the millions of dollars of funding as a cannabis micro - enterprise.

The truth is, without state restriction in the requirements for obtaining a cannabis license, New Jerseyans have to compete with out-of-state operators with experience and millions of dollars in funding, which could potentially take them out of the industry.

NJ's cannabis microbusiness license can help level the field, giving New Jersey exclusivity to a scaled-down version of the industry and securing the participation of state-resident small business owners in the cannabis market.

If you're interested in getting started with opening a dispensary in New Jersey or starting a growing operation in the Garden State, here's everything you need to know about the New Jersey cannabis microbusiness license and how to apply for it.

The New Jersey Microbusiness license is a stripped-down version of one of the cannabis licenses available in NJ, which in addition to the normal provisions, includes additional protection for New Jersey citizens, giving them, some leverage to enter the cannabis industry. Four classes of cannabis licenses are open for micro-versions of dispensaries, growers, processors or wholesalers.

New Jersey cannabis regulations state that the characteristics of the microbusiness license are:

10% of cannabis licenses must be issued to micro-enterprises.

Micro business owners must be New Jersey residents who have resided in New Jersey for the past 2 years;

51% of the owners of the micro-enterprise must be resident in the neighboring city or municipality where the micro-enterprise will operate.
No owner, director, officer or other person with a financial interest who also has the decision-making authority for an authorized cannabis establishment, distributor or delivery service, regardless of whether it is a micro-enterprise or

not, can hold any financial interest in a micro-enterprise

" The commission must ensure that at least 10 percent of the total licenses issued for each class of cannabis establishment, or for cannabis distributors and cannabis delivery services, are designated and issued to micro-enterprises only, and that at least the total licenses issued must be issued to micro-enterprises. "

Types of cannabis micro - enterprise licenses in New Jersey

Class 1 - Cannabis growers, a micro enterprise can grow cannabis with a canopy growing area of no more than 2,500 square feet; 24 feet high and 1,000 plants.

Class 2 - Cannabis Processors / Producers, a micro enterprise can process no more than 1,000 pounds of dried cannabis per month;

Class 3 - Cannabis wholesalers, a micro enterprise can wholesale no more than 1,000 pounds of dried cannabis (or equivalent in other forms) per month;

Class 4 - Cannabis distributor - all.

Class 5 - Cannabis retailers, a micro-enterprise may purchase no more than 1,000 pounds of dried cannabis or equivalent in other forms for retail per month.

Class 6 - Delivery - all.

" Microbusiness " defined by the New Jersey cannabis law:
" MicroBusiness " means a person or entity authorized by the Cannabis Regulatory Commission as cannabis grower, cannabis manufacturer, cannabis wholesaler, cannabis distributor, retailer of cannabis or cannabis delivery service."

How much are the licensing costs of the New Jersey cannabis micro - enterprise license

The maximum fee for issuing or renewing a license designated and issued to a micro enterprise must not exceed half the rate applicable to a license of the same class issued to a person or entity that is not a micro enterprise. A license designated and issued to a micro enterprise is valid for one year and can be renewed annually.

CHAPTER 24: GROWING MARIJUANA

Industrial hemp is the fastest growing crop in American agriculture. The US defines industrial hemp as cannabis sativa plants containing 0.3% or less of THC. Prior to 2015, hemp was virtually non-existent in terms of U.S. agriculture, because the Federal Controlled Substances Act prevented it.

Then, in 2014, a new agricultural law opened the industrial cultivation of hemp in experimental form and for pilot programs controlled by the state. The following year, 1,500 acres of hemp were planted in the United States. Today, after hemp was removed from federally controlled substances thanks to the latest Farm Bill of 2018, according to new data from the United States Department of Agriculture (USDA), crops have increased 100-fold and have reached 146 thousand acres, about 60 thousand hectares. To make a comparison throughout Europe, 47 thousand hectares were cultivated in 2017.

In 2018, hemp was planted in 18 states and in 2019 that more than doubled, with 37 states growing it for a 350% increase in acreage in December 2018. Leading the way is Montana (over 44,000 acres), which has more than double the area of the second state - Colorado - when it comes to growing hemp.

Meanwhile, the US Department of Agriculture is rolling out a new pilot hemp insurance program, which will provide Actual Production History coverage under the agency's Multi- Peril Crop Insurance program. The new insurance program adds to federal crop insurance, which the USDA said hemp growers will have access to in August.

And another step concerns the US Environmental Protection Agency, which has approved the use of 10 pesticides for the cultivation of hemp, nine of which are biopesticides and one is a conventional pesticide. Four of the biopesticides approved are produced by Agro Logistic Systems, Inc. and they all contain neem oil. Three are produced by Hawthorne Hydroponics, and two are produced by Marrone Bio Innovations; both are fungicides.

Growing Marijuana in Canada

On October 17, 2018, Canada legally regulated cannabis for adult and non-medical use. While the federal government has retained control over production, it has given individual provinces and territories the responsibility of regulating retail sales in their respective territories.

The stated purpose of the legal regulation was to protect young people, promote public health and reduce crime in the drug markets. This report analyzes how different provinces have tried to achieve these results and what different regulatory models have been applied. We focus on how the regulations have been applied to the production, sale and marketing of cannabis products.

Production

Federal regulations establish two classes of production license: a "grow" license, which authorizes holders to grow cannabis, and a "processing" license, which authorizes holders to produce cannabis-based products (such as edibles). There are also "micro-cultivation" and "micro-processing" licenses, which authorize the cultivation and production of cannabis on a small scale. All holders of cultivation and processing licenses are subject to federal controls in relation to the safety of the premises, aimed at reducing the risk of cannabis theft for the purpose of diversion from the legal market, as well as to encourage good production practices and quality controls of products.

There are power limits for certain products. For example, food products are limited to 10 mg of THC for "immediate container" (the outer package) and in case a package contains two or more units, these must in any case reach up to a maximum of 10 mg of THC in total. Particularly dangerous products (such as those intended for use in the west) are totally prohibited. The content and types of products can be further limited at the provincial level. For example, Quebec has moved to ban certain types of edibles that could appeal to children (including cannabis brownies, chocolate and gum) from being sold on the market.

Sale

According to Statistics Canada, in the first six months following the legalization of cannabis, the federal government raised CAD 55 million (1 CAD about 0.64 EUR) in both excise and property taxes, while provincial governments raised $. 132 million. The licensing regime differs between provinces and depends on whether it applies to brick-and-mortar stores or online sales. In all cases, the limit allowed for personal possession in public is 30 g of dried cannabis.

Provinces / Territories Age limit

In-store sales

Online Sales

Limits of possession

Alberta. 18 Private licensed stores. Public 30g cannabis (in public)

No limits in the house

British Columbia. 19 Private and Public Licensed Stores. Public 30g cannabis (in public)

1000g at home

Manitoba. 19 Private licensed shops. Private 30g cannabis (in public)

No limits in the house

New Brunswick. 19 Public Shops. Public 30g cannabis (in public)

No limits in the house

Newfoundland and Labrador. 19 Private licensed shops. Public 30g cannabis (in public)

No limits in the house

Northwest Territories. 19 Public Shops. Public 30g cannabis

No limits in the house

Nova Scotia. 19 Public Shops. Public 30g cannabis

No limits in the house

Nunavut. 19 None. Private 30g cannabis (in public)

No limits in the house

Ontario. 19 Private licensed stores. Public 30g dry cannabis

No limits in the house

Prince Edward Island. 19 Public Shops. Public 30g cannabis

No limits in the house

Quebec. 21 Public Shops. Public 30g cannabis

150g at home

Saskatchewan. 19 Private Licensed Stores. Private 30g cannabis

No limits in the house

Yukon. 19 Private licensed shops. Public 30g cannabis

No limits in the house

All provinces have designated government agencies that oversee the regulation of retail markets. In most cases, these are the agencies that already have the responsibility of controlling the legal alcohol market.

Some provinces have adopted a government-run retail store system, while others allow private companies to apply for a retail license. License holders are therefore subject to provincial regulations.

In Ontario, the provincial government has implemented an initial limit of 25 retail licenses across the province. This has since been gradually lifted, partly due to under- supply issues, but also as part of a phased approach. As part of this, the province has also limited the amount of retail licenses that can be awarded to each applicant (be it an individual or a company).

As of February 2020, Alberta had the largest number of retail stores in operation (415). Except for the Northwest Territories, no other province or territory recorded more shops per resident. This may be partly due to the relatively cheap licensing costs. In British Columbia, the cost of applying to open a retail store is $ 7,500 and an additional $ 1,500 for the first year of licensing and each year of renewal. In contrast, in Alberta, the application fees are only $400 while the license fee is $ 700.

The location of retail stores is also subject to regulation. In Ontario, the regulations specify the maximum number of retail stores allowed in each area of the province. In Saskatchewan, the provincial government attempted to encourage out-of-town retail stores by offering reduced annual licensing rates: $ 3,000 for a store in one city, and $ 1,500 for a store outside the city.
Licensing for retail stores is also subject to municipal zoning requirements, and local municipalities may decide to ban them entirely. While this helps to ensure that local communities have an influence on how cannabis retailing operates in their area, it risks inhibiting access to legal cannabis markets for consumers in areas

where no shops are allowed, or where there are very few. Ontario has tried to counter this by providing $ 40 million over two years to "help municipalities ... for the actual costs of legalizing recreational cannabis," allowing more funds to be allocated to municipalities that have not banned shops. However, overall cannabis availability remains patchy: as of July 2019, the average distance for Canadian residents to reach the nearest cannabis shop was 34km.

Marketing and design

Product marketing is strictly federally regulated. The Cannabis Act prohibits the promotion of cannabis to young people, through endorsements or otherwise associating the use of cannabis with "glamor, entertainment, excitement, life, risk or daring". Likewise, products are prohibited from creating the impression of possible "health benefits or cosmetics" (except when dealing with licensed medical products).

Federal cannabis regulations stipulate that containers must be opaque or translucent; they must prevent cannabis from being contaminated; they must keep cannabis dry (if it is dry cannabis); have a guarantee (i.e. a seal or blister) that proves that the product has not been previously opened; be childproof; and must not contain more than 30 g of dried cannabis (or equivalent). Additionally, regulations prohibit bright or eye-catching packaging in ways that somewhat reduce the visibility of important health information required about the product. Health warnings are posted on the Canadian government website and amended from time to time, with regulations requiring these messages to be displayed in rotation on containers to ensure equal recognition.

Consumption and possession

Under federal laws, adults are allowed to have up to four cannabis plants per residence. In most provinces, this limit is maintained, but domestic cultivation is regulated. Conversely, Quebec and Manitoba have tried to ban home growing entirely. Federal regulation also allowed provinces to individually determine access age thresholds and, in all but two provinces (Quebec and Manitoba), the minimum age for buying and owning cannabis is set locally at the minimum age for alcohol. The federal limit for possession of no more than 30 grams of dried cannabis is unchanged across all provinces. However, the provinces have tried to limit cannabis use. In Ontario, cannabis can be smoked or vaped on sidewalks and parks (although this may be limited by municipalities over time). Conversely, smoking or chewing cannabis is prohibited on sidewalks in Saskatchewan and in parks in British Columbia. Prohibiting consumption on (or near) school properties is a common restriction, although it is also prohibited in Québec to possess cannabis inside school or university buildings (except student residences). In British Columbia, if people consume cannabis (even in ways other than smoking or vaping) on a school property, the education authority, superintendent, and principal are each held accountable. This is to ensure that school authorities are encouraged to enforce consumer laws.

32 IDEAS TO MAKE MONEY IN THE CANNABIS INDUSTRY

The cannabis market has become known as a very profitable market to enter and many people are looking for ways to satisfy consumers in this market so that they can make a profit for themselves. Legalization of cannabis is fueling tremendous growth in the global marijuana industry. As the most diverse medicinal plant in the world, it really comes as no surprise that entrepreneurs are capitalizing on it. You too can join this trade. If you reside in the United States, here are some business ideas that can allow you to profit from the cannabis industry.

1. Start a Cannabis Farm.

With cannabis gaining approval in more states of the United States, now may be the time to start a cannabis farm so you can supply users. Called the green run, if you can start now, you'd probably be ahead of the herd. Growing marijuana or cannabis can be more of a chore than growing a regular plant, so it's important to keep up to date on knowledge. You will need to understand the conditions necessary for plants to thrive and how to care for your plants as they grow. Marijuana production requires a license, so you'll need to know the application process in your state.

2. Process Cannabis.

Much marijuana production is done by large companies, but there are many consumers who prefer a product that has been personally processed in a distinct and controlled environment. Marijuana processing is a good choice for anyone who is not interested in growing or cultivating plants, but knows how to dry, store and package the product for various uses. In most states, you need to be licensed to handle marijuana, so find out what the requirements are where you live.

3. Start a Marijuana Delivery Business.

Marijuana or cannabis is a medicinal plant that must always be in a controlled environment if you want to keep all of its components intact. If you live in a state that has legalized the use of both recreational and medical marijuana, you can start a marijuana transport and delivery business. First you will need to contact local farms or dispensaries and become an expert on the best places to purchase particular strains of the plant. You should also know people or companies that need the supplies as they would be the ones making the payments. Since marijuana or cannabis is not a bulky product to carry, you may not have to worry about acquiring a van for the company; a motorcycle or even a bicycle would help you get started, depending on how you want to start. Note that you need to register the activity before you can do anything else. After completing your registration, you can now start promoting your services and start looking for businesses and individuals to deliver to.

4. Sell edible marijuana snacks.

Not everyone likes smoking, and with the quit-smoking promotions in the US, many people are quitting smoking. But that doesn't mean people who don't smoke don't use marijuana. They just eat it instead of burning it. If you have great culinary skills, you can start baking and selling snacks that are seeded with cannabis. Start with a few articles and then grow your business as your popularity grows. You can start with cannabis tea, chestnuts, cakes, pies, etc. And sell them to your specialized clients.

5. Make Marijuana-Based Body Products.

Marijuana as a plant has many beneficial properties for almost every aspect of human existence. Since marijuana has some healing and restorative properties for the skin, you can start a company where you make creams, lotions, soaps, massage oils, etc. with marijuana in. This business would be easier for you to get started if you already have a similar business, as you just need to add the plant to your ingredient list. This doesn't mean you can't start from scratch if you want, it would just take you longer. Even renowned actress Whoopi Goldberg started her line of medical marijuana items, including baths, body balms, and more.

6. Open a cannabis accessories shop.

If you are still skeptical about handling or treating the marijuana leaf directly, you can save yourself the stress by selling accessories for the use of marijuana. This means things that can be used for marijuana consumption such as pipes, bongs etc. Or things that contain marijuana messages like t-shirts, dog collars, and anything else you can make or buy. You would do well in this area if you are handy with crafts. You can also start reselling marijuana accessories that you pick up in stores or flea markets. Buy these cheap, clean them, and then advertise them. You can also search online stores like eBay for these items, and you may even need to open your own online store to maximize sales.

7. Organize Marijuana Parties.

Yes, there is such a thing as marijuana parties. This is not actually a party where attendants would be drowned in marijuana, but a party that has a marijuana theme, all of which reminds you of weed. Marijuana parties are a growing trend across the country, and many people include cannabis in celebrations such as weddings, reunions, and birthday parties. You can get involved in this part of the industry by selling your experience as a party planner or event coordinator. Alternatively, you can plan these parties and invite like-minded people to join for a fee.

8. Become a Canadian Florist.

Traditional florists and people with a keen eye for arranging beautiful bouquets have started adding cannabis to their creations. A cannabis flower display is a perfect gift for someone special and can be a wonderful addition to weddings and other celebrations. If you know how to handle flowers, you should look into this growing trend. You can use weed to grow your florist business as many floral entrepreneurs have done because people are still curious about the plant and the reputation surrounding it has also started to decline, thus making the industry more accessible to many people.

9. Become a Marijuana Products Trader.

As mentioned earlier, the cannabis plant has many medical properties and the products made with them are quite effective. Due to the low popularity of the industry currently, companies are looking for people to help build awareness about their products and help them explode the myths about weed. If you are a marketer who knows your way around social media and other media, you can start marketing marijuana related products. You need to contact companies to let them know that you are willing to promote their products and you can discuss remuneration with them. If you are experienced enough in the industry, you could make it big in a short time.

10. Become a cannabis consultant.

Are you an expert on the cannabis plant, have you done a lot of research on this plant, have you worked with these plants for many years? If you answered yes to these questions, you can become a cannabis plant consultant. You can set up your own business and use the benefit of your knowledge to help small business owners understand their products, customers, and processes. Many people want to get into the industry, but they often don't know much about the business or the plant itself. They will pay you for your knowledge of various strains, processing techniques or growing procedures. There are of course many legal regulations governing the way cannabis is produced, managed and sold. There are also regulations on how cannabis is marketed, where it is consumed and much more. And, if you happen to live in the United States, these regulations can radically change from one state to another. This is what you should help your customers with. People would be willing to pay the maximum dollar for this type of service.

11. Become a Cannabis Dealer.

Retail is a line of business that every product goes through before reaching consumers. Depending on the state you reside in, you can become a cannabis dealer by selling cannabis products. You can do this in a showcase setup with basic products. If you want to become a successful cannabis retailer, you should make your store look like something that almost anyone can walk into and feel comfortable with. This is because the image that surrounds cannabis is that it is only used by drug addicts. Your lively, clean, friendly, well-lit shop should help to dispel such thoughts and help you welcome many new customers.

12. Make cannabis cosmetics.

Cannabis has also found a place in the cosmetics industry, and it's really doing very well. A lot of research is underway and many cosmetics are produced courtesy of this plant. In fact, there is research showing that compounds like THC and

CBD (pain relief, anti-inflammation, etc.) can be administered locally via balms, sprays, lotions, and more. You can also go deeper into this research and start producing your own range of cannabis-infused cosmetics highlighting their protective and healing properties.

13. Open a Marijuana / Cannabis Seed Bank.

Since the use of marijuana has been legalized in some states of the United States, many people have been looking forward to owning their own plants. In order to own a plant, they must have a seed with which to sprout it; you can create a cannabis seed bank to meet this need. To open a marijuana / cannabis seed bank, you must first ensure that the market exists in your locality. Once that is ascertained, you need to be on the lookout for where to buy viable seeds and also how to market your business. You should make sure you know so much about the plant so that you can educate your buyers.

14. Open a cannabis restaurant.

Like drugs and cosmetics, there are myriad ways in which you can integrate cannabis into your food and make the most of it. If you know all the ways to use cannabis to improve the taste of a meal, you can open your own cannabis-themed restaurant. To manage this business, you may need to contact the marijuana plant regularly, but if you have any personal or legal issues with this, you can use concentrates as they can also give you what you need.

15. Start a Cannabis Concentrate Mining Business.

Another large part of the legal cannabis business revolves around the extraction and sale of cannabis concentrates. These concentrates are used in various industries, from cosmetics to medical to the catering industry. If you are able to start this business, you will not know where to distribute your concentrates as the industry is still quite young. You can decide to carve out a niche for your business and extract concentrates that can only be used in a particular industry. Know that to maximize profits in the industrial sector, your business should be in an area with many cannabis farms so that have easy access to raw materials.

16. Develop machinery for extracting concentrates.

Instead of making concentrates yourself, you may decide to manufacture machinery that can be used for extraction. This is one of those cannabis businesses that do not require contact with the leaf. You can get this equipment, stock up on it, and sell it for a slightly higher price than what you paid for it to make a profit. While the initial investment will be quite high, the returns will amply compensate for it.

17. Immerse yourself in the art of cannabis.

The cannabis industry has supported the rise of a group of fantastic artists who have created everything from glassware to paintings of all kinds. If you are artistic, you can start creating cannabis-inspired art. Cannabis has even made its way into high fashion and traditional fast fashion, with single pieces costing thousands. Currently, the art world is experiencing a major resurgence of weed-inspired designs across all disciplines. Find out where your skills fit and take them from there.

18. Start a cannabis-inspired bed and breakfast.

With regulations having been relaxed on cannabis use, many cannabis users are looking for places where they can find similar minds especially when traveling. If you happen to live in one of these relaxed cannabis territories, you might think about hosting the perfect smoking-friendly bed and breakfast. If you have free space, you can decorate the place according to what you think cannabis lovers might find suitable and offer something special. You may also be able to sell some homemade cannabis edibles on the side to excite your guests and make more money.

19. Become a cannabis event planner.
From weddings and birthday parties to educational seminars and product launches, a cannabis event planner can help a wide range of clients with bespoke services. You should be ambitious, charismatic and have an eye for detail to effectively run a pot party and to attract the right kind of customers.

20. Run a cannabis catering company.
If you've been in the system and have advice on how to infuse cannabis into anything edible, you can start a cannabis catering company. Take catering to a whole new level by preparing cannabis-inspired menus with cannabis- infused drinks, appetizers and gourmet appetizers, such as cannabutter- marinated steak. If you have the skills, why not profit from them.

21. Host Cannabis Painting Classes.
A painting class is a social gathering where people of like minds come together to paint and discuss or enjoy things that are common to them. The same principle can be applied here. If you live in a society that has people with similar interests, you can bring them together by organizing a painting class

where they can paint and enjoy snacks, drinks and fun times.

22. Become an Authorized Cannabis Distributor.

There are also some states where retail companies and other companies that want to sell cannabis products have to go through distributors. So this is another potential business opportunity for those who want to manage product sales to businesses in certain states. You can become a licensed distributor.

23. Produce Safe Packaging for Marijuana Products.

The marijuana plant needs careful and controlled storage to stay fresh and effective all year round. This means that the products require specialized packaging. If you are in the packaging business, you can start making packaging for marijuana products manufactured by other companies. Retailers and other businesses also need protective, child-resistant packaging solutions that keep products fresh.

24. Become a cannabis-related app developer.

There are many possibilities for mobile apps related to the cannabis industry as well, from those that locate dispensaries to those that provide information or even social features to users. You can identify a niche and develop apps that can be of great help in the industry.

25. Be a Founding Partner of a Social Network.

You can also potentially start your own social network aimed specifically at cannabis users. This could also present some unique advertising opportunities for other cannabis companies as it can be a way to bring producer and consumer together. if you dive into this industry early, your social network could grow in popularity in a short time.

26. Become a Related Software Developer.

As the cannabis industry is relatively new, the companies involved still have a long way to go when it comes to finding the exact tools that really meet their needs. Restaurants, retail stores, and other types of businesses all have software programs made specifically to help them perform essential business functions. So if you are a software developer, you can potentially do the same for the cannabis industry.

27. Become a cannabis product reviewer.

Currently, many cannabis-related products are hitting the market and consumers are now inundated with choice. So you could potentially build a business around providing reviews and other relevant information to help consumers make informed decisions about the products they want to use. As there aren't many people in this service, you can easily get noticed for brand sponsorships.

28. Become a tour guide.
If you live in a place that has become a destination for cannabis users, you can also potentially offer a tour guide service where you take people to relevant destinations in your city or state.

29. Start a Cannabis Subscription Service.
This is a great business idea that can help consumers offer a continually new variety of cannabis products once they hit the market. Offering these boxes is also a great service that can be provided not only to individual subscribers but also to large scale cannabis events, for festivals, even as a welcome gift in a cannabis themed hotel or bed and breakfast. You can put together your box service to deliver things like cannabis-related snacks, paper rolls, cannabis stickers and magazines, pipes, and more. You can even use it as a cannabis gift service where you offer cannabis-

related gifts to people at the request of your customers.

30. Become a commercial lender of cannabis.

Because of the somewhat unpopular nature of the cannabis industry, many companies related to cannabis have difficulties in accessing funds for their activities. If you have some money to spare and are looking for a profitable investment opportunity, you can start lending to cannabis-related businesses in exchange for interest. If you don't want to work within the industry but just want a good return, this may be a possibility for you.

31. Start a Cannabis Placement Service.

As the cannabis industry is relatively new and requires some specialization and experience to work in the industry, it may be difficult for related companies to find staff. You could launch a cannabis placement service where you will have to match industry-experienced job seekers with companies that need their services. This sector may be slow for now, but it has been billed to gain momentum over the next few years.

32. Run a cannabis blog.

With the cannabis industry growing with great momentum, people are looking for as much information as possible about this plant and its products. If you are an expert in this area, you can start a blog dedicated to the cannabis industry. Here, you could inform your readers about new legal developments, new products and services etc. You can even run product reviews, job postings and even company reviews.

www.ingramcontent.com/pod-product-compliance
Lightning Source LLC
Chambersburg PA
CBHW071356210526
45465CB00001B/112